Mastering Math through Magic

Grades 6-8

* * * * * * * * * * *

Mary A. Lombardo

LINWORTH
LEARNING

A Publication of Linworth Learning

Linworth Publishing, Inc.
Worthington, Ohio

Library of Congress Cataloging-in-Publication Data

Lombardo, Mary A.
    Mastering math through magic, grades 6-8 / Mary A. Lombardo.
        p. cm.
    Includes bibliographical references and index.
    ISBN 1-58683-137-2
    1. Magic tricks in mathematics education. 2. Mathematics--Study and teaching (Middle
school) I. Title

    QA20.M33L665 2003
    372.7'044--dc21

                                                        2003043572

Published by Linworth Publishing, Inc.
480 East Wilson Bridge Road, Suite L
Worthington, Ohio 43085

Copyright © 2003 by Linworth Publishing, Inc.

ISBN: 1-58683-137-2

5 4 3 2 1

Table of Contents

✳ ✳ ✳ ✳ ✳ ✳ ✳ ✳ ✳ ✳

Math Skills Cross Reference Chart

Trick	Trick Title	Page	Addition	Subtraction	Multiplication	Division
1	Movie Magic: Just for Fun!	10				
2	Three Steps to Magic	12	X			X
3	Summing It Up	14	X		X	
4	Half Track	17	X	X	X	X
5	Number Split	19	X	X	X	X
6	The Final Answer	21	X	X	X	X
7	Pick a Date	24	X	X	X	
8	Clock Moves	26	X			
9	Adding Five	28	X	X	X	
10	Clockworks	31	X	X	X	X
11	Five Across	33	X	X		X
12	Birthday Bash	35	X	X	X	
13	What's Your Number?	38	X	X	X	X
14	Double Dice Magic	40	X	X	X	
15	Tricky Threesome	42	X	X	X	
16	Takeaway Dice	44	X	X		
17	Three Timing Dice	46	X	X	X	X
18	Pocket Change to Spare	49	X	X	X	
19	Money Piles	51	X	X	X	
20	Hide and Seek	54	X	X	X	
21	Square Coins	56	X	X	X	X
22	Knowing the Unknown	59	X	X	X	
23	A Double Dose	61	X	X	X	X
24	X Marks the Spot	63	X	X	X	X
25	Minus the Magic	65	X	X	X	X
26	I Know Where You Live!	68	X		X	X
27	Magic Multiples	70			X	X
28	What Time Did You Say?	72	X	X	X	X
29	Fractured Fractions	74	X	X	X	
30	Act Your Age	76	X	X		
31	Age Old Magic	78	X	X	X	
32	Cross Out	80	X	X	X	
33	Writing Practice	83			X	
34	Six Nines Equals What?	83				
35	Predictably Perfect	84	X	X		
36	Prediction Ploy	86	X	X		
37	Mysterious Facts about the Number Nine	88				

How to Use This Book

* * * * * * * * * *

The Math Skills Cross Reference Chart

The Math Skills Cross Reference Chart on page iii gives the reader an at-a-glance look at which magic tricks apply to each of the math skills listed. The name of the math trick as well as the page on which it is found are listed, and an X indicates that the math skill is represented by the trick.

Be a magician yourself!

Start the unit by performing some of the tricks and impress your class with your magical powers. The directions for the tricks are written in easy-to-follow, step-by-step directions and most of the props you will use are already in your classroom or home.

Present the student introduction.

Use the teacher script as a student introduction to stimulate class interest in learning to do the magic tricks.

Review the basic math operations that are listed here.

Many of the magic tricks are based on the basic operations that follow. Practicing these operations will make the reasoning behind the tricks easier to understand.

1. Doubling a number and then dividing it in half brings back the original number.

To double a number, you multiply it by 2. To halve a number you divide it by 2.

Example:

$6 \times 2 = 12$ (doubling)

and

$12 \div 2 = 6$ (halving)

2. Adding an odd numbered group (3, 5, 7, etc.) of evenly spaced numbers together and then dividing the sum by how many numbers you added gives you the center number.

Example:

$7 + 11 + 15 = 33$

There are three evenly spaced numbers.

$33 \div 3 = 11$

11 is the center number.

3. If you have three evenly spaced numbers, subtracting the amount between the numbers from the third number and adding it to the first number gives you three numbers equal to the center one.

Example:

7, 11, 15 are spaced four numbers apart

$15 - 4 = 11$ and $7 + 4 = 11$

4. Multiplying a number by 10 gives you the number plus a zero.

Example:

$3 \times 10 = \underline{3}0$

$5 \times 10 = \underline{5}0$

5. To find an unknown variable in an algebraic equation dealing with addition, subtract the known variable from the answer of the equation.

Example:

$x + 5 = 25$

$25 - 5 = 20$

$x = 20$

6. To find the unknown variable in an algebraic equation dealing with subtraction, add the known variable to the answer of the equation.

Example:

$x - 7 = 29$

$29 + 7 = 36$

$x = 36$

Once you've reviewed and practiced operations, it's time to get into the magic!

Start with the tricks in the first chapter. The answers to these tricks are always the same and the math reasoning is easy to understand.

Learning the easiest tricks first will pave the way for attempting more challenging tricks. Choose a trick and perform it for the class. Ask the students how they think the magic works. Test any ideas to see if they are correct.

Go over the directions step by step, either by reading them to the students or by copying the directions for use on an overhead projector and reading them together. The students should practice the trick in pairs or small groups and, if no correct theories have been advanced, again asked if anyone can guess what makes the trick work.

After reading the explanation of how the trick works found under the heading "Why does this work?" ask the students to write the equations they used to make the trick work.

Copy and distribute the student handout. Complete the "How did you do?" section together, with students writing the answers in their own words. Continue in this manner with the remainder of the tricks.

Teacher Introduction

✳ ✳ ✳ ✳ ✳ ✳ ✳ ✳ ✳ ✳

The successful completion of most magic tricks depends a great deal on diversion. A skilled magician will divert the audience's attention so tricks can be performed without anyone seeing or deducing exactly what is happening.

Mastering Math through Magic uses diversion too. As students focus on learning magic tricks, they don't realize that they are improving their knowledge of how numbers work along with practicing basic math skills. The book provides a fun way to review and practice math skills for everyday use as well as for the math and reading testing that is federally mandated in grades 3 through 8.

Each trick in this book also uses some form of diversion so that, even though the tricks themselves are simple, the audience cannot guess how the magic is performed.

You can use this book in several ways:

- You can use the tricks to practice math skills in the classroom with every student "checking" to see that the math done by the magician and volunteer is correct.
- You can present a simple or an extravagant magic show.
- You can give individual students the directions for a trick and the time to perform it in class as a fun reward for some job well done.

The National Council of Teachers of Mathematics (NCTM) suggests that teachers should present students with activities that will interest and challenge them as well as help them develop a sense of numbers. By using the tricks in this book, you will be following that suggestion.

Organization of the Book

After this introductory section for the teacher, there is a short teacher script to help introduce the magic unit to the students. Seven chapters of tricks follow. Each chapter begins with a listing of tricks that follow and the math skills they cover as well as a teacher script for introducing the chapter and teaching the tricks.

Chapter I includes tricks that should be done one time only in any magic presentation as the answer in each trick is always the same. The tricks in Chapter II use calendars and clocks, while those in Chapter III involve the use of dice. Coins are the basis of the magic in Chapter IV, and Chapter V uses basic algebraic equations to trick the audience. Chapter VI is an assortment of tricks that don't fit in any of the prior categories, and Chapter VII, the last chapter of tricks, deals with the magic of the number nine.

Then the magic begins! The tricks are written in easy-to-follow, step-by-step instructions to facilitate instruction. Each trick begins with a short introductory statement for the students to use to announce what they plan to do. The tricks themselves are organized in a three-part format.

1. **THE PROPS** tell what materials are needed to do the trick.
2. **THE TRICK** gives step-by-step directions for performing the trick with suggestions for what the students should say.
3. **THE MAGIC** explains how the trick works mathematically.

Examples are included to help the teacher explain how the tricks work and to make performing and understanding the tricks easier.

At the end of each trick, there is a student handout with some questions under the heading "How did you do?" which the students should answer in their own words. This exercise gives them the opportunity to review what they have done and write the math equations they used to demonstrate they understand the math reasoning behind the trick.

Objectives

This book was written with the following objectives in mind:

1. Correlate teaching and learning activities with the concepts contained in the math standards as set forth by the National Council of Teachers of Mathematics.

The National Council of Teachers of Mathematics has developed a set of ten standards for math learning from pre-kindergarten through grade 12. The tricks in *Mastering Magic through Magic* correlate with the concepts in these standards.

2. Demonstrate that working with numbers can be fun.

When students look forward to presenting magic tricks, they approach the task with pleasure, not fear, and build confidence in their abilities to work with numbers.

3. Cultivate a sense of numbers.

Number sense is a familiarity with how numbers work. Students with number sense can predict what will happen in number situations and have increased flexibility when working with numbers.

4. Increase fluency in mental manipulation of numbers.

As students become more familiar with the logical way that numbers work, they will be able to do many math functions mentally.

5. Show the relationships between number operations.

Many of the tricks depend on reversing operations to make the "magic" work. Students see that addition and subtraction, multiplication and division, and doubling and halving are opposites.

6. Provide an opportunity for students to write about what they have done and learned.

Research shows that writing about math operations cements understanding. After each trick there is a section for students to write about the performance and to review the mathematical reasons and equations that make the trick work.

7. Improve confidence in one's knowledge of numbers by successfully participating in performance of magic tricks.

Subject matter is best learned and remembered through play. Students are focused on mastering a magic trick so they are more relaxed about learning. Complexity of the tricks varies so all children are challenged and can participate successfully.

Correlation with National Math Standards

The math concepts presented through the magic tricks in *Mastering Math through Magic* correspond to those presented in the math standards issued by the National Council of Teachers of Mathematics for students from preschool through grade 12. In the listings that follow the corresponding math concepts are shown in bold print.

For a complete description of the Math Standards, refer to the NCTM Web site at <www.nctm.org>.

Correlation of Magic Tricks to Math Concepts

NUMBER AND OPERATIONS: All of the tricks correlate with this concept.
The math which underlies the "magic" in each trick demonstrates how numbers and number relationships work. Because each trick involves performing math operations, the tricks also encourage facility and accuracy in computing.

PROBLEM SOLVING: All of the tricks correlate with this concept.
After each trick is performed and before the math explanation is read, students are asked to formulate a mathematical theory of why the magic works. As they theorize about the math operations used in the tricks, they use problem-solving techniques and build and review mathematical knowledge.

REASONING AND PROOF: All of the tricks correlate with this concept.
The students conjecture about how the tricks work mathematically and evaluate their guesses to determine if they can prove they are correct.

COMMUNICATION: All of the tricks correlate with this concept.
After each trick, the students must complete a handout explaining in their own words the math that makes the magic work. Their communication must be clear and they must demonstrate that they understand the math reasoning.

CONNECTIONS: All of the tricks correlate with this concept.
All of the tricks with the exception of Movie Magic use interconnecting mathematical ideas and operations. The connections between division and multiplication, subtraction and addition, and doubling and halving are clearly shown.

REPRESENTATION: All of the tricks correlate with this concept.
The math operations in all of the tricks can be represented pictorially or by using objects.

If You Decide to Present a Magic Show

✳ ✳ ✳ ✳ ✳ ✳ ✳ ✳ ✳ ✳ ✳

Putting on a magic show does not have to be a big production. You have many options.

OPTION 1. The easiest way to have a magic show is to assign one trick to each student and to present the tricks within your own classroom. The advantages for doing it this way are:
- students have a chance to perform in front of a familiar audience;
- all students practice math skills as they check to see that the magician and the volunteer are doing the math operations correctly;
- the magicians can explain the math process to their classmates, providing another opportunity to review skills and thought processes.

OPTION 2. Another fairly easy way to put on a show is to divide your class into several groups with each group learning and performing a variety of tricks.

OPTION 3. The most time-consuming way to have a show is for each student in your class to learn one or more tricks and, as a whole, perform for other individual classes or at a school assembly. If your class has organized and presented a show at your school, you may want to share the magic with others at senior citizen centers, retirement homes, or libraries.

Learning how to perform the tricks can be done during the school day or can be assigned for homework or a combination of both.

The Props

Most of the tricks call only for paper and marker. Use a large piece of paper posted where the audience can see it and a dark-colored marker so the audience can easily check to make sure the volunteers are following the directions and doing the math correctly, and that the magicians have done exactly what they said they would do.

Other simple props are regular dice, a clock or picture of a clock face, coins, stones or dried beans, and some pages from a calendar, preferably a large wall calendar so that they can be posted for the audience to see.

With tricks that use small objects, such as coins or beans, it is a good idea to use an overhead projector so the audience can see what is going on in the trick. If this is not possible, make sure the magician keeps the audience informed about what is happening.

In Chapter III: Calendars and Clocks, you will need to cut out a box that can be laid over a calendar page to show a box of 15 numbers, 5 numbers across and 3 numbers down, on the calendar. This is the only prop that has to be made.

The Dress

If your students are to perform in front of an audience, they will naturally be concerned about what they will wear. Ask the children to recall magicians they have seen perform and describe what they wore.

Some magicians are very casual, wearing everyday clothes. Some magicians wear robes and turbans, some wear tails and top hats, and others wear nice suits or dresses. Pairing black pants and a black shirt makes another common "magician" outfit.

The important thing to stress to your students is that whatever they choose to wear must be comfortable. If they have to worry about how their clothes fit, or if their clothes have to be adjusted constantly, the students won't be able to concentrate on performing the tricks.

Your students may want to wear more exotic costumes like capes, bow ties, top hats, and turbans. These costumes are easily made.

Making Costumes

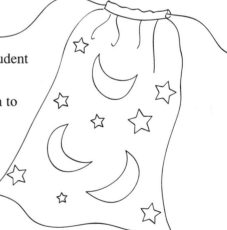

To make the cape:
1. Measure enough black crepe paper or cloth to cover the back of the student twice from shoulder to shoulder.
2. Hem one end of the material and thread a long ribbon through the hem to gather the cape.
3. Attach star stickers and larger stars and moon cutouts made from the aluminum foil with pieces of double-sided tape.

To make a top hat:
1. Cut a doughnut shape from black oak tag, the center of which fits on the student's head. This will be the hat's brim.

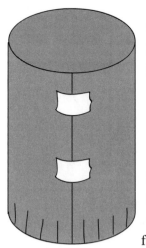

2. Tape a large piece of construction paper into a cylinder, fitting it into the circle you have cut with about two inches showing below the brim. Cut it down a few inches if it is too tall. Cut slits all around the end that is below the brim.

3. Fold up the cut pieces and glue them onto the bottom of the brim.

4. The costume can be completed by fashioning a bow tie from crepe paper of any color and voila! Instant magician!

To make a turban:

1. Take a piece of cloth, a scarf, or a piece of crepe paper about four feet long and a foot wide. Drape it over the front of the head then bring the ends up and crisscross them around the back of the head, then around the front, as far as they will go and tuck the ends under. A star sticker or aluminum foil cutout can be taped to the front of the turban.

The Patter

A magic show is not just about doing magic tricks. The magician will want to put the audience in a receptive frame of mind and one of the best ways to do this is to tell jokes or relate amusing incidents that have happened.

Students can research joke books to find some jokes that are suitable to use, or they can recall personal stories and practice telling them aloud.

The students will also have to create their own magic words to use as they perform their tricks. These can be alliterative or rhyming phrases or anything that sounds magical.

When they are learning the tricks, the students should also practice how they will give the directions for doing the tricks. Each trick includes suggested statements that the students can read, or they can make up their own patter as they work through the tricks.

Practice is very important. You cannot emphasize this point enough. The students should practice the jokes; they should practice what they will say throughout the tricks; they should practice performing the tricks; and, if they will be wearing any kind of costumes, they should have at least one practice wearing their costumes.

Teacher Script for Student Introduction

In the weeks to come we are going to be learning to perform some magic tricks. The tricks that you're going to learn will be easy for you to do, but it will be hard for your friends to figure out how you work your magic. Some of the tricks you will do are very simple and some are more challenging, but, I promise you, they are all puzzling and astonishing!

Getting Started

If you've watched some of the great magicians perform, you know that they don't just stand up and perform magic tricks. They tell the audience what to expect before they do the tricks and tell a few jokes or stories to get everyone laughing and in a good mood.

Successful magicians rehearse and rehearse before they perform. They don't just practice their tricks. They also practice what they will say to the audience. You will want to do the same thing. Choose some jokes you like and memorize them. Practice telling the jokes and talking about what you will do in the tricks. Do the tricks several times before you perform them for an audience.

Another thing to remember is you shouldn't say the answer to the trick too fast. Scratching your head and rubbing your chin and frowning, as if you are thinking very hard before saying some magic words and revealing the answer, will make the tricks seem more mystifying.

The Language of Magic

Magicians often use words that sound magical just before they demonstrate their magic powers. "Abracadabra, hocus pocus" are some famous magic words that you've probably heard many times. Where do the magical words come from? The magicians make them up. Just like famous magicians, you can make up and use any magic words you like. Try some rhymes like,

"Beetle juice and bat's wings,

I am the master of magical things."

Or just string some words together that start with the same letter and sound good like,

"Suffering saliva and salamander soup."

What Do Magicians Wear?

What should you wear when you perform? Some magicians wear capes and top hats, some dress in everyday clothes. You could dress in a special outfit, something that you don't usually wear to school, or you can borrow or make clothes that you think would be just the thing for a magician to wear. If you decide you want to make a special outfit, I can help you with some ideas.

Whatever outfit you decide on, make sure you are comfortable in it and don't worry about looking like a magician. Your tricks will show you are a real magician no matter what you are wearing.

Learning the Magic Tricks

The tricks we are going to learn are organized so that they are easy to learn and perform. The instructions tell what props are needed and then detail step by step how the trick is done. Each trick begins with one sentence that you can use to announce what you will be doing in the trick. There are also some suggestions for what to say to your audience during the trick.

Many of the directions for doing the tricks are short and easy so you will be able to memorize the steps. Some of the tricks have more involved directions so you may want to copy the steps onto small index cards that you can read from as you perform the trick.

Finally, in a section called "The Magic," there is an explanation, for our eyes only, of how the trick works, and a place for you to write about how you performed the trick.

Now, on to the magic!

Chapter I
ONE-TIMERS

✳ ✳ ✳ ✳ ✳ ✳ ✳ ✳ ✳ ✳

Teacher Notes

There are six tricks in this chapter. The answer to each trick is always the same so these tricks, if presented in a magic show, should be performed only once. Variations are suggested for some of the tricks, giving the students the opportunity to make up their own magic tricks. All of the tricks are easy to perform and understand.

Trick 1. Movie Magic: Just For Fun!
The magician will predict what number someone will end up with after writing several number words and the corresponding numbers.

Trick 2. Three Steps to Magic: Addition, Division
The magician gives the correct answer after someone has changed a secret three-digit number to a two-digit number.

Trick 3. Summing It Up: Multiplication, Addition
The magician will be able to predict the final answer to a math problem which is all about dates.

Trick 4. Half Track: Multiplication, Addition, Division, Subtraction
The magician will be able to tell the final answer after a volunteer chooses a secret number and changes it through multiplication, addition, division, and subtraction.

Trick 5. Number Split: Multiplication, Addition, Subtraction, Division
A secret number is changed several ways, but the magician will be able to tell what the final number is.

Trick 6. The Final Answer: Addition, Subtraction, Multiplication, Division
This trick begins with someone's age and ends with the magician telling what the final number is.

✳ ✳ ✳ ✳ ✳ ✳ ✳ ✳ ✳ ✳

Teacher Script

The first magic tricks you will learn are tricks that you should perform only once each time you do your magic tricks. They are great for warming up an audience, but the answer to each trick is always the same. If you perform them more than once, the audience will probably guess how the magic works, and you want to keep that your secret. Some of the tricks, however, have variations listed that will change the trick so that they can be performed again.

Remember that each trick is followed by an explanation of what makes it work. Before we read the explanation, we'll take a few minutes to try to figure out the secret ourselves. But don't worry. Even if you can figure it out, your audience will not be able to. That's because, when you perform magic tricks in a show, you don't give the audience time to think about anything. You perform one trick after another with very little time between tricks. Your magic secrets will be safe.

Now we're ready to perform magic.

Movie Magic: Just for Fun!

Explanation to the audience: **I am going to predict what number you will end up with after you have done some work with the letters in the name of your favorite movie.**

THE PROPS

a dark-colored marker

a large piece of paper

a small piece of paper

THE TRICK

1. Write the number 4 on a small piece of paper and give it to someone in the audience to hold. Explanation to the audience: **This is my prediction for the final answer to the number work you are going to do.**

2. Give a volunteer the marker and ask him or her to write down the name of his or her favorite movie.

3. Instruction to the volunteer: **Count the number of letters in the movie name and write that number down.**

4. Instruction to the volunteer: **Now write the word for the number you just wrote.**

5. Instruction to the volunteer: **How many letters are in that word? Write that number down.**

6. Keep asking the volunteer to write the word for each number and then the number of letters in each word until he or she cannot go any further. It will be when he or she reaches 4.

7. Ask the person in the audience who is holding your prediction to open the paper and read the number you have written there—4.

THE MAGIC

Four is the only digit with a value that equals the number of letters in the word.

Why does this work?

No matter how many letters the volunteer starts with he or she will always end up with the number four.

Example:

Favorite Movie:	The Lord of the Rings
Number of Letters:	17
Spell the Word:	Seventeen
Number of Letters:	9
Spell the Word:	Nine
Number of Letters:	4
Spell the Word:	Four
Number of Letters:	4

Movie Magic: Just for Fun!

Name _____ Date _____

Now you try it:

1. Write the name of your favorite movie.
2. Count the letters in the words and write that number.
3. Spell the number word.
4. Count the letters and write that number.
5. Spell the number.
6. Keep doing this until you can't go any further. Four will be the last number you get.

How did you do?

Materials (What props did you use?)

Procedure (How did you do the trick?)

Conclusion (What makes the trick work?)

Equations (What equations did you use to make the magic work?)

Variation

Try this trick by starting with a very long number like one million seven hundred fifty thousand four hundred fifty-three. Then try it with the number fourteen. Do the work on the back of this paper.

Three Steps to Magic: Addition, Division

Explanation to the audience: **I will be able to tell you the answer after you change a three-digit number to a two-digit number.**

THE PROPS
a dark-colored marker

a large piece of paper

THE TRICK
1. Give a volunteer the marker and put on your blindfold.
2. Instruction to the volunteer: **Write a three-digit number where all the digits are the same.**
3. Instruction to the volunteer: **Add the digits and divide the original number by the sum of the digits.**
4. Say some magic words and reveal: **The number you are left with is 37.**

THE MAGIC
Why does this work?

When you add three identical digits and divide the original three-digit number by their sum, the answer will always be 37.

Example:

Write a three-digit number with the digits all the same:	777
Add the digits:	$7 + 7 + 7 = 21$
Divide the original number by the sum of the digits:	$777 \div 21 = 37$

As the numbers get larger, the sum of the numbers also gets larger, but the ratio is always the same. Three 3's equals 9 into 333, three 4's equals 12 into 444, three 5's equals 15 into 555. Notice the divisors grow by 3 while the dividends grow by 111.

111 divided by 3 = 37. The answer will always be 37 if you use a three-digit number.

Three Steps to Magic: Addition, Division

Name _____ Date _____

Now you try it:

1. Write a three-digit number with all the digits the same.
2. Add the digits. Divide the original number by the sum of the digits.
3. Is your answer 37? If you did the math correctly, it is.

How did you do?

Materials (What props did you use?)

Procedure (How did you do the trick?)

Conclusion (What makes the trick work?)

Equations (What equations did you use to make the magic work?)

Variations

Do this trick with four-digit numbers where the digits all the same: 7777, 5555, 3333, 9999. Add the digits and divide the original number by the sum of the digits. What is the answer? Is it the same in each the equation no matter what number you choose? Why? What is the original ratio? Do the work on the back of this paper.

Summing It Up: Multiplication, Addition

Explanation to the audience: **I will predict the correct sum to numbers we haven't picked or added up yet.**

THE PROPS

a dark-colored marker

a large piece of paper

a small piece of paper

THE TRICK

1. Double the number of the present year and write it on a piece of paper. Give it to a member of the audience to hold.
2. Instruction to the volunteer: **The number I have written on this paper is my prediction for the answer to the number problem we are going to do.**
3. Give the marker to a volunteer. Instruction to the volunteer: **Please write down the year you were born.**
4. Instruction to the volunteer: **Please write, below that in a column, the year when something important happened to you.**
5. Instruction to the volunteer: **Please write below that how old you will be on your birthday this year.**
6. Instruction to the volunteer: **Please write below that the number of years that have passed since the important event you thought of in Step 4.**
7. Ask him to add up the four numbers.
8. Instruction to the audience: **Would the person who is holding my prediction please unfold the paper and read the number out loud?**
9. It will be the same as the sum of the numbers that have just been added.

THE MAGIC

The answer to this trick will always be double the number of the current year no matter how old or young the volunteer is!

Example:

1990	Born
1995	Learned to ski
13	Age by the end of this year
+ 8	Years since that special event
4006	

Look at the example above. If it is the year 2003, the four years the volunteer chose add up to 4006.

Why does this work?

The year when the volunteer was born plus his or her age this year adds up to the number of the current year.

In the example the volunteer was born in 1990 and will be 13 years old at the end of this year. Those two numbers add up to 2003.

1990	The year the volunteer was born
+ 13	How old the volunteer will be at the end of this year
2003	

The year when the important event happened and the number of years since then also add up to the current year.

1995	When the volunteer learned to ski
+ 8	Years since then
2003	

So that is two times the current year, which is exactly the prediction you made!

$$2003 \times 2 = 4006$$
or
$$2003 + 2003 = 4006$$

Summing It Up: Multiplication, Addition

Name _____ Date _____

Now you try it:

1. Write down the year you were born.
2. Now write down the year something special happened to you.
3. Next, write down how old you will be at the end of this year.
4. For your final number, write down how many years it has been since the special event.
5. Add these four numbers. Is your answer the same as 2 times the number of the current year? It is if you added and subtracted correctly!

How did you do?

Materials (What props did you use?)

Procedure (How did you do the trick?)

Conclusion (What makes the magic work?)

Equations (What equations did you use to make the magic work?)

Variation

Change this trick so you can do it again by adding another important event and the age of the volunteer when it happened. Then your answer will be three times the current year. Do the work on the back of this paper.

Half Track: Multiplication, Addition, Division, Subtraction

Explanation to the audience: **After you choose a number and change it several times, I will tell you the number you end up with!**

THE PROPS

a dark-colored marker

a large piece of paper

THE TRICK

1. Put on your blindfold and ask a volunteer to pick any even number up to 100 and write it on the paper.
2. Instruction to the volunteer: **Multiply your number by 2 and then add 112.**
3. Instruction to the volunteer: **Split your answer in half.**
4. Instruction to the volunteer: **Now split that number in half.**
5. Instruction to the volunteer: **Subtract half your original number.**
6. Say some magic words and reveal: **You have ended up with the number 28.**

THE MAGIC

If the steps are followed exactly as you read them, the answer to this puzzle will always be 28.

Why does this work?

In this trick you start with any even number and double it. You split that number and the 112 that was added two times. That means that the 112 is cut down to 28 (half of 112 is 56 and half of 56 is 28). The original number was doubled. When that is cut in half the first time, you have the number back. When you cut it in half the second time, you have half of it. So, when you subtract half the original number, you are left with 28.

Example:

Pick 68:	68
Multiply it by 2:	136
Add 112:	248
Divide it by 2:	124
Divide it by 2 again:	62
Subtract half your original number:	62 – 34 = 28

The answer is 28, just as you said!

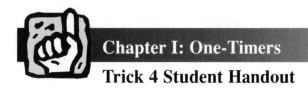

Half Track: Multiplication, Addition, Division, Subtraction

Name _____ Date _____

Now you try it:

1. Pick any even number up to 100.
2. Multiply it by 2.
3. Add 112.
4. Divide it by 2.
5. Divide it by 2 again.
6. Subtract half of the original number you picked.
7. If you followed the steps in order, your answer is 28.

How did you do?

Materials (What props did you use?)

Procedure (How did you do the trick?)

Conclusion (What makes the magic work?)

Equations (What equations did you use to make the trick work?)

Variation

Try this trick choosing a number up to 1,000. Follow the same pattern. Does the trick work the same way? Do the work on the back of this paper.

Number Split: Multiplication, Addition, Subtraction, Division

Explanation to the audience: **I will be able to tell you the number you end up with after you pick a number and change it in six ways.**

THE PROPS
a dark-colored marker, a large piece of paper

THE TRICK
1. Put on a blindfold and ask a volunteer to pick a number and write it on the paper.
2. Instruction to the volunteer: **Multiply your number by 2.**
3. Instruction to the volunteer: **Add 5 and then add 24.**
4. Instruction to the volunteer: **Subtract 9.**
5. Instruction to the volunteer: **Split the answer in half.**
6. Instruction to the volunteer: **Subtract the number you started with and tell me when you are done.**
7. Say some magic words and reveal the answer. It will always be 10.

THE MAGIC
Knowing that doubling and halving are opposite functions makes this trick easy.

Why does this work?

In this trick, you have someone multiply a number by 2 which is the same as doubling and then split the answer in half. Doubling and halving will bring the original number. When the original number is subtracted, the volunteer is left with half of the numbers you gave.

Example:

5 + 24 = 29

29 − 9 = 20

20 split in half = 10

The answer will always be 10.

You can change this trick by substituting other numbers, but you will have to work out what the answer will always be before you perform the trick.

Example:

Pick 7:	7
Multiply it by 2:	14
Add 5:	19
Add 24:	43
Subtract 9:	34
Split in half:	17
Subtract the number you started with:	17 − 7 = 10

Follow the steps in order and the answer will always be 10.

Number Split: Multiplication, Addition, Subtraction, Division

Name _____ Date _____

Now you try it:

1. Pick a number. Multiply it by 2.
2. Add 5. Then add 24.
3. Subtract 9 and split the number in half.
4. Subtract the number you started with. Your answer is 10.

How did you do?

Materials (What props did you use?)

Procedure (How did you do the trick?)

Conclusion (What makes the magic work?)

Equations (What equations did you use to make the trick work?)

Variation

Here's a similar trick. Someone picks a number from 100 to 500, adds 33, multiplies that number by 2, subtracts 40 and splits the answer in half. Then he or she subtracts the number picked in the first place. To get his or her answer, you double 33, subtract 40, then divide that in half. Can you explain why this trick works? Look for the same numbers for a clue. Do the work on the back of this paper.

The Final Answer: Addition, Subtraction, Multiplication, Division

Explanation to the audience: **Although I don't know how old you are, I will be able to tell you the number you end up with after you change your age in several ways.**

THE PROPS

a dark-colored marker

a large piece of paper

a small piece of paper

THE TRICK

1. Ask for a volunteer who is older than 9, but who does not have two of the same digits in his or her age. For instance, the trick will not work with someone who is 22 or 66.
2. Put on your blindfold. Instruction to the volunteer: **Write down your age, then reverse the digits and subtract the smaller number from the larger one.**
3. Instruction to the volunteer: **If there are two digits in the answer, add them and multiply the answer by 10. If there is only one digit, multiply that by 10.**
4. Instruction to the volunteer: **Now multiply the answer by 5.**
5. Instruction to the volunteer: **For your last step, divide that number by 2.**
6. Say some magic words and then reveal: **You have ended up with the number 225.**

THE MAGIC

This is a trick where you have complete control of the numbers at all times because you know what number the volunteer will reach when he or she reverses his or her age and subtracts the smaller number from the larger one.

Why does this work?

When a two-digit number is reversed and the smaller number is subtracted from the larger one, the remaining digit or the sum of two remaining digits will be 9. Nine times 10 is 90. Ninety times 5 is 450. Four hundred fifty divided by 2 is 225.

Example:

Write down 27.

Reverse it to 72 and subtract the smaller number from the larger one ($72 - 27 = 45$).

Add the two digits in 45 to get 9 ($4 + 5 = 9$).

$9 \times 10 = 90$

$90 \times 5 = 450$

$450 \div 2 = 225$

The Final Answer: Addition, Subtraction, Multiplication, Division

Name _____ Date _____

Now you try it:

1. Write down any age between 10 and 100 that does not have two of the same digits.
2. Reverse the numbers and subtract the smaller from the larger.
3. If there are two digits in the answer, add them.
4. Multiply the last number by 10 and then multiply the answer by 5.
5. Divide the answer by 2 and your answer should be 225.

How did you do?

Materials (What props did you use?)

Procedure (How did you do the trick?)

Conclusion (What makes the magic work?)

Equations (What equations did you use to make the trick work?)

Variation

Explain why you can't do this trick with an age that contains two of the same numbers. Now try the trick using the age 107. You will have to change one step in the trick. Which one is it? Hint: you are working with three digits. Do the work on the back of this paper.

Chapter II
CALENDARS AND CLOCKS

✳ ✳ ✳ ✳ ✳ ✳ ✳ ✳ ✳ ✳ ✳
Teacher Notes

The tricks in this chapter use calendars and clocks and work because the numbers on both are in numerical order.

Trick 7. Pick a Date: Multiplication, Addition, Subtraction
The magician will be able to tell what date is picked from a calendar.

Trick 8. Clock Moves: Addition
The magician will know the number someone is pointing to on a clock.

Trick 9. Adding Five: Multiplication, Addition, Subtraction
The magician will be able to tell the sum of three columns of five numbers each on a calendar, after only being told one number.

Trick 10. Clockworks: Subtraction, Addition, Division, Multiplication
The magician correctly tells the answer after a volunteer finds the difference between two numbers on a clock and changes it through division and multiplication.

Trick 11. Five Across: Addition, Division, Subtraction
After being told the sum of five numbers which someone has chosen on the calendar, the magician will know what five dates were picked.

Trick 12. Birthday Bash: Multiplication, Addition, Subtraction
The magician will accurately tell the volunteer's month and day of birth.

✳ ✳ ✳ ✳ ✳ ✳ ✳ ✳ ✳ ✳ ✳
Teacher Script

A calendar is a great prop to use for some very puzzling magic tricks. That's because calendars are arranged in a very orderly fashion. The numbers are in numerical order and numbers above and below each other are exactly seven numbers apart.

Clocks are good for magic tricks too because they, like calendars, have a very orderly arrangement. There are 12 numbers in numerical order and opposite numbers that are 6 spaces apart.

Pick a Date:
Multiplication, Addition, Subtraction

Explanation to the audience: **You will pick a date on the calendar and I will be able to tell you what date you picked.**

THE PROPS

a large wall calendar, a dark-colored marker, a large piece of paper

THE TRICK

1. Give a volunteer the marker and put on your blindfold.
2. Instruction to the volunteer: **Circle a day on the calendar and write that number on the paper.**
3. Instruction to the audience: **Double the number and add 18.**
4. Instruction to the audience: **Multiply the number by 5 and add 12.**
5. Instruction to the audience: **Tell me the answer and I will tell you the date you picked.**
6. In your mind, cross out the digit in the ones place and subtract 10 from the rest of the number and you will know what date the volunteer chose.

Figure 2.1 Calendar

THE MAGIC

The volunteer doubles the date and then multiplies it by 5. This is just like multiplying it by 10 so he or she ends up with a zero after his or her date.

Example: 12 x 2 = 24; 24 x 5 = 120

Why does this work?

Once the number is multiplied by 10 we know that the digit in the ones place no longer has anything to do with the number he or she chose. The date chosen is in front of the zero.

He or she added 18 before he or she multiplied by 5. Five times 18 is 90. Then he or she added 12. Adding the digits in the tens place, 9 and 1, we end up with 10.

When you are told the volunteer's final answer, cross out the digit in the ones place and subtract 10 from the rest of the number and you will know what date the volunteer chose.

Example:

Choose 26:	26
Double it:	52
Add 18:	70
Multiply by 5:	350
Add 12:	362

Cross out the digit in the ones place and you are left with 36.

Subtract 10:   36 – 10 = 26, the date chosen in the first step!

Pick a Date:
Multiplication, Addition, Subtraction

Name _____ Date _____

Now you try it:

1. Choose a date from the calendar. Double the number and add 18.

2. Multiply the answer by 5 and add 12.

3. Cross out the digit in the ones place and subtract 10.

4. You should be right back where you started at the date you picked.

How did you do?

Materials (What props did you use?)

Procedure (How did you do the trick?)

Conclusion (What makes the magic work?)

Equations (What equations did you use to make the magic work?)

Variation

Follow the pattern but try adding numbers other than 18 and 12. Calculate what you added in the tens place and above to know what to subtract to get the date the volunteer picks. Do the work on the back of this paper.

MAY						
					1	2
3	4	5	6	7	8	9
10	11	12	13	14	15	16
17	18	19	20	21	22	23
24	25	26	27	28	29	30
31						

Clock Moves: Addition

Explanation to the audience: **I will tell you what number you are pointing to after you move around the clock clockwise and counterclockwise.**

THE PROPS

a clock or picture of a clock

THE TRICK

1. Hang the clock where the audience can see it, choose a volunteer, and put on your blindfold.
2. Instruction to the volunteer: **Put your finger on a number on the clock.**
3. Instruction to the volunteer: **Move your finger six hours going either way around the clock.**
4. Instruction to the volunteer: **Now move counterclockwise a number of hours that is equal to the hour you first picked.**
5. Instruction to the volunteer: **Now move clockwise five spaces.**
6. Say some magic words and reveal: **You are now pointing at the number 11.**

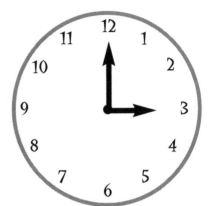

Figure 2.2 Clock

THE MAGIC

Why does this work?

If the volunteer did not move six spaces in the first step, this is how this trick would work. He or she picks a number and moves counterclockwise a number equal to the hour he or she picked. Let's say he or she picks 3 o'clock and moves counterclockwise to number 12. You tell him to move five spaces clockwise. This brings him or her to the number 5. In your mind, you add 6 and know that he or she is at the number 11.

Moving six spaces around the clock in the first step is just to confuse the volunteer. Because six spaces around the clock is opposite the hour that was picked, the trick is not changed.

Example:

Choose 5 o'clock. Move six spaces to 11 o'clock.

Move counterclockwise a number of spaces equal to the hour picked, 5 o'clock. This brings you to 6 o'clock.

Now move your finger five spaces clockwise.

Add 6 to 5 to get 11, the hour the volunteer is now pointing at.

Clock Moves: Addition

Name _____ Date _____

Now you try it:

1. On the clock to the right, put your finger on an hour.
2. Move your finger six spaces either way around the clock.
3. Move counterclockwise a number of spaces equal to the hour you chose in Step 1.
4. Now move five spaces clockwise.
5. Add 6 and 5 to get 11. Your finger is now pointing at 11 o'clock.

How did you do?

Materials (What props did you use?)

Procedure (How did you do the trick?)

Conclusion (What makes the magic work?)

Equations (What equations did you use to make the magic work?)

Variation

This trick can be done many times by changing the number of spaces you tell the volunteer to move in the last step. If you say move six spaces then you add 6 plus 6 and know that the answer is 12 o'clock. Try it using at least three other numbers. Do the work on the back of this paper.

Adding Five: Multiplication, Addition, Subtraction

Explanation to the audience: **Now I will add five columns of three numbers each without even looking at the numbers! And I will get the right answer every time!**

THE PROPS

a calendar

a paper to lay over the calendar so that five rows of three numbers each show

a few pieces of transparent tape

a small pad and pencil

THE TRICK

1. Give a volunteer the cut out paper and tape and turn your back. Don't put on a blindfold as you may want to use a pad and pencil to record your answers.

2. Instruction to the volunteer: **Tape the cardboard over the calendar so that five rows of three numbers each are showing. Tell me the first number in the box and I will tell you the sum of each column of numbers.**

3. When the volunteer tells you the first number, add 9 to get the center number. Multiply the center number by 3 to get the sum of the middle column. Write that number down.

4. Then subtract 3 from that answer to get the sum of the second column and subtract 3 to get the sum of the first column. Write those down too.

5. Now add 3 to your first answer to get the sum of the fourth column and 3 to that answer to get the sum of the fifth column. Write them down.

6. Say some magic words and reveal the sum of each of the five columns.

7. Ask someone from the audience to add each column to prove you are right!

❀ **MAY** ❀						
					1	2
3	4	5	6	7	8	9
10	11	12	13	14	15	16
17	18	19	20	21	22	23
24	25	26	27	28	29	30
31						

Figure 2.3

THE MAGIC

The numbers above and below each other on a calendar are evenly spaced, seven numbers apart. In a column of three numbers, when you subtract 7 from the bottom number and add it to the top number, you have three numbers all the same as the middle number. That is why multiplying the middle number by 3 will give you the sum of the column.

28

Example:

In the numbers 5, 12, 19, multiplying the middle number, 12, by 3 is the same as adding all three numbers. 12 x 3 = 36 and 5 + 12 + 19 = 36.

Why does this work?

Adding 9 to the first number brings you over two spaces and down one space to the center number. You multiply the center number by 3 to get the sum of the center column.

By adding 3 to that number you get the sum of the fourth column of numbers and adding 3 again gives you the sum of the last column. By subtracting 3 from the center sum, you get the sum of the second column, and subtracting 3 again gives you the sum of the first column.

Example:

12	13	14	15	16
19	20	21	22	23
26	27	28	29	30

First add 9 to 12 to get 21, the center number. Then multiply the center number by 3 to get the sum of the center column. The center number is 21 and 3 x 21 = 63. Now you know that the sum of that column is 63 (14 + 21 + 28 = 63).

Because there are three numbers in each column, each one less than the number after it, you subtract 3 from 63 to get 60 for the sum of the second column (13 + 20 + 27 = 60) and 3 again to get 57 for the sum of the first column (12 + 19 + 26 = 57).

Because there are three numbers, each one more than the numbers they follow, you add 3 to 63 to make 66 for the sum of the fourth column (15 + 22 + 29 = 66) and 3 again to get 69 for the sum of the final column (16 + 23 + 30 = 69).

The five sums are 57, 60, 63, 66, 69.

Adding Five:
Multiplication, Addition, Subtraction

Name _____ Date _____

Now you try it:

1. On the calendar to the right, choose and circle any box of three numbers down and five numbers across.

2. Add 9 to the first number to get the center number and multiply it by 3.

3. Subtract 3 from the answer twice to get the sum of the second and first columns.

4. Add 3 to the answer twice to get the sum of the fourth and fifth columns.

MAY

					1	2
3	4	5	6	7	8	9
10	11	12	13	14	15	16
17	18	19	20	21	22	23
24	25	26	27	28	29	30
31						

How did you do?

Materials (What props did you use?)

Procedure (How did you do the trick?)

Conclusion (What makes the magic work?)

Equations (What equations did you use to make the magic work?)

Variation

See if you can work this trick with seven numbers across. How will you find the sum of the two extra columns? Do the work on the back of this paper.

Clockworks: Subtraction, Addition, Division, Multiplication

Explanation to the audience: **I will get the right answer to the work you do with numbers even though you will not tell me what numbers you start with.**

THE PROPS

a clock or a drawing of a clock

a dark-colored marker

a large piece of paper

THE TRICK

1. Ask for a volunteer and show them the clock, then turn your back.
2. Instruction to the volunteer: **Please choose two opposite numbers on the clock and write them on the paper.**
3. Instruction to the volunteer: **Subtract the smaller number from the larger. Then add 34 to the remainder.**
4. Instruction to the volunteer: **Divide that number by 2.**
5. Instruction to the volunteer: **Now multiply your answer by 3.**
6. Instruction to the volunteer: **Subtract 5 from your answer and tell me when you are ready.**
7. When the volunteer has the answer, say some magic words and reveal that the answer is 55.

Figure 2.4 Opposite Numbers on a Clock Face

THE MAGIC

Because you know that the difference between opposite numbers on a clock is always 6, it's easy to get the answer to this trick.

Why does this work?

There are 12 hours on the clock.

Opposite numbers are half of the clock away from each other so they are half of 12, which is 6. You know the number they start with!

Then the volunteer adds and subtracts numbers you give them so you are always in control of what the answer will be.

The answer is always 55 in this trick if you use the numbers given.

If you decide to change the numbers, figure out what the new answer will be before you do the trick.

Example:

The volunteer starts with the number 6.

Then 34 is added:	$6 + 34 = 40$
The answer is divided by 2:	$40 \div 2 = 20$
That answer is multiplied by 3:	$3 \times 20 = 60$
The last step is to subtract 5:	$60 - 5 = 55$

Clockworks: Subtraction, Addition, Division, Multiplication

Name _____ Date _____

Now you try it:

1. Choose two numbers opposite from each other on the clock and subtract the smaller one from the larger one.
2. Add 34 to that answer. Divide your new answer in half.
3. Multiply your answer by 3. Subtract 5. Is the result 55?

How did you do?

Materials (What props did you use?)

Procedure (How did you do the trick?)

Conclusion (What makes the trick work?)

Equations (What equations did you use to make the magic work?)

Variation

Instead of 34 add a different even number. Determine what the answer will be before you do the trick. If you added 26, what would the answer be? _____ 48? _____ 72?_____ 14? _____?

Do the work on the back of this paper.

Five Across: Addition, Division, Subtraction

Explanation to the audience: **Without looking, I will be able to tell what five numbers you pick from a calendar.**

THE PROPS

a page from a calendar

a crayon

THE TRICK

1. Give a volunteer the calendar page and the crayon and put your on blindfold.
2. Instruction to the volunteer: **Circle any five dates in a row. Add those five numbers and tell me the sum. I will then tell you the five numbers you picked.**
3. Divide the number the volunteer gives you by 5.
4. That number and the two numbers right before it and the two numbers right after it are the five numbers the volunteer picked. Say some magic words and reveal the numbers the volunteer chose.

Figure 2.5

THE MAGIC

Why does this work?

This trick works because the numbers on the calendar are in numerical order.

The volunteer picks five numbers in order, adds them, and tells you the sum. When you divide the sum of five numbers in numerical order by 5, the answer will be the middle number. Because the numbers are one number apart, the two numbers before the middle number and the two numbers after it are the correct dates.

Example:

Using the numbers 12, 13, 14, 15, and 16, we see that

12 + 13 + 14 + 15 + 16 = 70 and 70 divided by 5 equals 14, the middle number.

The two numbers before 14 are 12 and 13 and the two numbers after 14 are 15 and 16.

Five Across:
Addition, Division, Subtraction

Name _____ Date _____

Now you try it:

1. Circle five consecutive numbers on the calendar.
2. Add the numbers and divide the answer by 5 to get the middle number. Subtract one twice to get the numbers before and add one twice to get the numbers after.

How did you do?

Materials (What props did you use?)

Procedure (How did you do the trick?)

Conclusion (What makes the magic work?)

Equations (What equations did you use to make the magic work?)

❀ **MAY** ❀						
					1	2
3	4	5	6	7	8	9
10	11	12	13	14	15	16
17	18	19	20	21	22	23
24	25	26	27	28	29	30
31						

Variation

Try this trick with any *odd amount of numbers*.

Pick seven numbers, add them, and then divide by 7. The answer and the three numbers right before it and the three numbers right after it will be the seven numbers.

What should you do if you pick three numbers? Do the work on the back of the paper.

Birthday Bash:
Multiplication, Addition, Subtraction

Explanation to the audience: **I will be able to tell you the month and day of your birthday.**

THE PROPS
a calendar

a dark-colored marker

a large piece of paper

THE TRICK

1. Give a volunteer the marker and calendar, put on your blindfold. Instruction to the volunteer: **Turn to the month of your birthday and circle the day of your birth on the calendar.**
2. Instruction to the volunteer: **Multiply the number of your birthday month by 5 and then add 7.**
3. Instruction to the volunteer: **Now multiply the answer by 4 and add 13.**
4. Instruction to the volunteer: **Now multiply by 5 and add the number of the day when you were born.**
5. Instruction to the volunteer: **Tell me the answer and I will tell you the month and day when you were born.**
6. You subtract 205 to give you three or four digits. The digit in the tens and ones places will be the day of birth. The other digit or digits will be the month of birth.

THE MAGIC

Why does this work?

The birthday month is multiplied by 5 and then by 4. This is like doubling it twice and multiplying it by 10. We know that when we multiply a number by 10 it gives us the number with a zero after it and doubling it makes it twice as large.

Example when the month is number 2:

$2 \times 5 = 10$ and $10 \times 4 = 40$

Then it's multiplied by 5 again. That gives us the original birth month with two zeroes:

$40 \times 5 = 200$

When the volunteer adds the number of the day of his or her birth, it takes the place of the zeroes. Say the birthday is the 26th:

$200 + 26 = 226$

The numbers we add, 7 and 13, are also multiplied to give us a total of 205:

$7 \times 4 = 28$ and $28 + 13 = 41$ and $41 \times 5 = 205$

Subtracting 205 gives us the numbers for the month and day of birth.

Note

In this trick, the months are numbered from 1 to 12 from January to December. You may want to write the correct number on each month on the calendar used for the trick.

Birthday Bash: Multiplication, Addition, Subtraction

Name _____ Date _____

Now you try it:

1. Circle the month and day of your birth on the calendar.
2. Multiply the number of your birthday month by 5 and then add 7.
3. Multiply the answer by 4 and add 13.
4. Now multiply by 5 and add the number of the day when you were born.
5. Subtract 205 to give you three or four digits. The digit in the tens and ones places will be the day of your birth and the other number or numbers will be the month of your birth.

❀ **MAY** ❀						
					1	2
3	4	5	6	7	8	9
10	11	12	13	14	15	16
17	18	19	20	21	22	23
24	25	26	27	28	29	30
31						

How did you do?

Materials (What props did you use?)

Procedure (How did you do the trick?)

Conclusion (What makes the magic work?)

Equations (What equations did you use to make the trick work?)

Variation

Try this trick by adding numbers other than 7 and 13. If you use 8 and 14, what number will you subtract to get the birth day and month? Do the work on the back of this paper.

Chapter III
DICE DOINGS

✳ ✳ ✳ ✳ ✳ ✳ ✳ ✳ ✳ ✳

Teacher Notes

Ordinary dice are used for all the tricks in this chapter. If you haven't any dice handy, don't worry. All the tricks can be done with someone choosing secret numbers.

Trick 13. What's Your Number? Multiplication, Addition, Division, Subtraction
The magician will be able to tell what number is rolled on one die.

Trick 14. Double Dice Magic: Multiplication, Addition, Subtraction
The magician will be able to tell what numbers are rolled on two dice.

Trick 15. Tricky Threesome: Multiplication, Addition, Subtraction
The magician will be able to tell what numbers are rolled on three dice.

Trick 16. Takeaway Dice: Addition, Subtraction
The magician will know what number was taken away after four dice have been rolled to make a four-digit number.

Trick 17. Three Timing Dice: Addition, Multiplication, Subtraction, Division
The magician will be able to tell someone the sum of the numbers rolled on three dice.

✳ ✳ ✳ ✳ ✳ ✳ ✳ ✳ ✳ ✳

Teacher Script

You've probably played a lot of games where you used dice. In the next few tricks you will be using dice again, but this time you will be performing magic tricks with the dice. The dice will be ordinary ones, just like you use in your games, but the tricks won't be ordinary at all.

Some of the tricks call for using paper and marker. Just as you did in some of the tricks you've already learned, you should have the volunteer do his or her work on a large piece of paper that the audience can see. Now it's time to roll some magic.

What's Your Number? Multiplication, Addition, Division, Subtraction

Explanation to the audience: **Without looking, I will correctly guess what number you roll on one die.**

THE PROPS

one die

a dark-colored marker

a large piece of paper

THE TRICK

1. Give a volunteer the marker and the die and put on your blindfold.
2. Instruction to the volunteer: **Roll a number and write it on the piece of paper.**
3. Instruction to the volunteer: **Double the number you rolled and add 28 to the answer.**
4. Instruction to the volunteer: **Divide that number by 2 and tell me your final answer.**
5. You will subtract 14 from the answer to get the number the volunteer rolled.

THE MAGIC

Why does this work?

When the volunteer doubles the number and then divides it by two, the volunteer is really doubling it and then splitting it in half. This gives the number rolled in the first place.

Since the volunteer split the number you gave (28) in half too, you subtract half of your number (14) and end up with the number rolled.

Example:

Roll a 6.

Six doubled is 12.

Add 28, which equals 40.

Divide that number by 2, which equals 20.

Subtract 14, and you are back at the number you rolled in the first place, 6.

What's Your Number? Multiplication, Addition, Division, Subtraction

Name _____ Date _____

Now you try it:

1. Roll a die. Write the number.
2. Double the number you rolled.
3. Add 28 to the answer.
4. Divide that number in half.
5. Subtract 14 and end up with the number you rolled in the Step 1.

How did you do?

Materials (What props did you use?)

Procedure (How did you do the trick?)

Conclusion (What makes the magic work?)

Equations (What equations did you use to make the magic work?)

Variations

Change this trick by adding a different even number. The magic works when you subtract half of whatever number you say to add. Try adding 48, 36, 18.

You can also do this trick without using dice. Follow the pattern and it will work even if you start the trick with one million. Try it and see. Do the work on the back of this paper.

Double Dice Magic: Multiplication, Addition, Subtraction

Explanation to the audience: **I won't look but I will know what two numbers come up when you roll dice!**

THE PROPS

two dice, a dark-colored marker, a large piece of paper

THE TRICK

1. Give a volunteer the dice and marker and put on your blindfold.
2. Instruction to the volunteer: **Roll two dice and write the numbers down.**
3. Instruction to the volunteer: **Pick one of the numbers and multiply it by 5.**
4. Instruction to the volunteer: **Add 9 to the product (the answer).**
5. Instruction to the volunteer: **Now double that answer.**
6. Instruction to the volunteer: **Now add the number on the other die and tell me the answer.**
7. In your head, subtract 18 from the number the volunteer tells you and tell the audience the two digits in your answer. They will be the two digits the volunteer rolled in Step 2.

THE MAGIC

Why does this work?

This works because multiplying a number by 5 and then doubling it is just like multiplying it by 10.

Example:

3 x 5 = 15 and 15 doubled is 30, and 3 x 10 = 30

When you multiply a number by 10, you always get the same number with a zero after it. For instance, 2 x 10 = 20 is 2 with a zero after it; 3 x 10 = 30 is 3 with a zero after it. When the volunteer multiplies one of the numbers by 5 and then doubles it, you have the first number rolled with a zero after it. Then add the second number, and you now have the two numbers rolled. The 9 is added just to fool the audience. Nine is added to the product and doubled in the next step. Nine doubled is 18, so when you subtract 18, you are just taking out what was put in.

You end up with the two numbers rolled. Actually, you can use any number you want in Step 5 as long as you subtract twice that amount to get the answer. For example, if 6 is added (instead of 9), just remember to subtract 12.

Example:

Roll a 4 and a 5.

Multiply one number by 5:	4 x 5 = 20
Add 9:	20 + 9 = 29
Double the answer:	2 x 29 = 58
Add the other number rolled:	58 + 5 = 63
Subtract 18:	63 – 18 = 45

4 and 5 are the numbers rolled.

Double Dice Magic:
Multiplication, Addition, Subtraction

Name _____ Date _____

Now you try it:

1. Roll two dice. Write the two numbers you rolled.

2. Multiple one of the numbers you rolled by 5.

3. Add 9 to the product and double the answer.

4. Add the number on the other die.

5. Subtract 18 from your answer.

6. Did you end up with the two numbers you rolled in the first place?

How did you do?

Materials (What props did you use?)

Procedure (How did you do the trick?)

Conclusion (What makes the magic work?)

Equations (What equations did you use to make the magic work?)

Variation

If you don't have any dice handy, you can do this trick without using dice. Choose any two numbers from 1 through 6. Follow the pattern and the trick will work for you. Do the work on the back of this paper.

Tricky Threesome: Multiplication, Addition, Subtraction

Explanation to the audience: **I will be able to tell you what three numbers come up when you roll the dice.**

THE PROPS

three dice

a dark-colored marker

a large piece of paper

THE TRICK

1. Give a volunteer the three dice and the marker. Put on your blindfold.
2. Instruction to the volunteer: **Roll three dice and write the numbers down.**
3. Instruction to the volunteer: **Double the number on the first die and add 3.**
4. Instruction to the volunteer: **Multiply that number by 5.**
5. Instruction to the volunteer: **Add the number of the second die and multiply the answer by 10. Add the number from the third die and tell me the final answer.**
6. In your mind, subtract 150 to get the three numbers that were rolled on the dice.

THE MAGIC

You work with one number at a time to get the three numbers that are rolled on the dice.

Why does this work?

The first number is doubled and then multiplied by 5. That's the same as multiplying it by 10, so you end up with the number with a zero after it in the ones place. Before it is multiplied by 5, 3 is added. The 3 is also multiplied by 5, giving you the number 15.

The second number is added to the first and is multiplied by 10, which again puts a zero in the ones place. That brings the 15 up to 150, which is what you subtract to get the three numbers rolled on the dice. Because you made sure there was a zero in the ones place before you added each number, you end up with the three numbers in the order they were added plus the 150.

Example:

Roll a 4, 5, and 6.

Double the 4 and add 3:	2 x 4 = 8; 8 + 3 = 11
Multiply the answer by 5:	5 x 11 = 55
Add the second number, 5:	55 + 5 = 60
Multiply by 10:	600
Add the third number, 6:	606
Subtract 150:	606 − 150 = 456
You have the three numbers rolled:	4, 5, and 6

Tricky Threesome:
Multiplication, Addition, Subtraction

Name _____ Date _____

Now you try it:

1. Roll three dice and write the numbers down.
2. Double the first number and add 3.
3. Multiply the answer by 5.
4. Add the second number and multiply that answer by 10.
5. Add the third number. Subtract 150. Now you have the original three numbers you rolled.

How did you do?

Materials (What props did you use?)

Procedure (How did you do the trick?)

Conclusion (What makes the magic work?)

Equations (What equations did you use to make the magic work?)

Variation

Try this trick with four dice. Follow the pattern but add one step. Because you have to make sure there is a zero in the ones place before you add a number, multiply the number by 10 before you add the fourth number. What will you subtract, 150 or 1,500? Do the work on the back of this paper.

Takeaway Dice: Addition, Subtraction

Explanation to the audience: **I will tell you the number that is taken away after four dice are tossed to make a secret four-digit number.**

THE PROPS

four dice

a dark-colored marker

a large piece of paper

THE TRICK

1. Give a volunteer the marker and the four dice and put on your blindfold. Ask the volunteer to toss the four dice on the table.
2. Instruction to the volunteer: **Arrange the dice in any order you want, making a four-digit number.**
3. Instruction to the volunteer: **Add the four digits and subtract the sum from the original number.**
4. Instruction to the volunteer: **Add 15 to the answer and cross out any one number except a zero.**
5. Instruction to the volunteer: **Tell me your final answer and I will tell you what number you took away.**
6. In your mind, or using a pad and pencil, add the digits in the number given to you and subtract 6. Then subtract the answer from the next multiple of 9. Your answer will be the number that was taken away.

THE MAGIC

The magic in this trick depends on the number you tell the volunteer to add.

Why does this work?

When the sum of the digits is subtracted from the number, the digits in the remainder will add up to 9.

Example: 4,532 − 14 = 4,518; 4 + 5 + 1 + 8 = 18; 1 + 8 = 9

The sum of the digits in the number you add, 15, equals 6 (1 + 5 = 6).

You know that whatever number remains after you take away the 6 has to add up to the next highest multiple of 9.

Example:

Roll a 3, 5, 6, and 2 to make the four-digit number 3,562.

Add the digits:	3 + 5 + 6 + 2 = 16
Subtract the answer from the original number rolled:	3,562 − 16 = 3,546
Add 15 to the number:	3,546 + 15 = 3,561
Take away one of the numbers:	Take away the 5 leaving 361
Add the three digits and subtract 6:	3 + 6 + 1 = 10 and 10 − 6 = 4
Subtract the answer from the next multiple of 9:	9 − 4 = 5
Five is the number that was taken away.	

Takeaway Dice: Addition, Subtraction

Name _____ Date _____

Now you try it:

1. Roll four dice to make a four-digit number.
2. Add the four digits and subtract the answer from the original number that was rolled.
3. Add 15 to the answer. Take away one digit (as long as it is not a zero) and add the remaining digits.
4. Subtract 6 from the answer and then subtract that answer from the next multiple of 9.
5. The answer will be the number that you took away.

How did you do?

Materials (What props did you use?)

Procedure (How did you do the trick?)

Conclusion (What makes the magic work?)

Equations (What equations did you use to make the magic work?)

Variation

Try this trick using 25 as the number you add instead of 15. Then subtract 7 in the next to last step instead of 6. Then try using 35 as the number you add. What number will you subtract? Do the work on the back of this paper.

Three Timing Dice: Addition, Multiplication, Subtraction, Division

Explanation to the audience: After you roll three dice and change the numbers several ways, I will tell you the sum of the numbers you rolled.

THE PROPS

three dice

a dark-colored marker

a large piece of paper

THE TRICK

1. Give a volunteer the marker and put on your blindfold.
2. Instruction to the volunteer: **Roll three dice, add the numbers, and double the answer.**
3. Instruction to the volunteer: **Add 24 to the answer.**
4. Instruction to the volunteer: **Subtract 8 and divide your new answer by 2.**
5. In your mind subtract 8 from the number the volunteer gives you. Say some magic words and reveal the sum of the three numbers the volunteer rolled.

THE MAGIC

Why does this work?

When the volunteer doubles the sum of the three dice and divides it in half he ends up with the number he or she started with. He or she adds 24 and subtracts 8. That leaves 16. Sixteen is also divided by 2 leaving 8. You subtract 8 to get the sum of the numbers he or she rolled.

Example:

Roll a 3, 4, and 5 and add the numbers:	$3 + 4 + 5 = 12$
Double the answer:	$2 \times 12 = 24$
Add 24:	$24 + 24 = 48$
Subtract 8:	$48 - 8 = 40$
Divide the answer by 2:	$40 \div 2 = 20$
Subtract 8 from 20 to get 12,	
the sum of the numbers rolled on the dice:	$20 - 8 = 12$

Three Timing Dice: Addition, Multiplication, Subtraction, Division

Name _____ Date _____

Now you try it:

1. Roll three dice. Add the digits.

2. Double the number and add 24.

3. Subtract 8.

4. Divide the new answer in half.

5. Subtract 8 again. You now have the sum of the three numbers rolled.

6. It's as simple as can be when you know what you're doing. Right?

How did you do?

Materials (What props did you use?)

Procedure (How did you do the trick?)

Conclusion (What makes the magic work?)

Equations (What equations did you use to make the magic work?)

Variation

Try this trick using more or fewer dice. Follow the pattern and see if it works the same way. Do the work on the back of this paper.

Chapter IV
MONEY MADNESS

✳ ✳ ✳ ✳ ✳ ✳ ✳ ✳ ✳ ✳

Teacher Notes

Because small objects are used in the following tricks, using an overhead projector is recommended in order to give the audience a good view of the magic that is happening in the trick. You will probably want to use a piece of clear plastic over the glass of the projector to protect it from scratching.

Trick 18. Pocket Change to Spare: Multiplication, Addition, Subtraction

The magician will be able to tell how much spare change a volunteer has.

Trick 19. Money Piles: Multiplication, Addition, Subtraction

Without looking, the magician will be able to tell how many coins are in each of two piles of coins.

Trick 20. Hide and Seek: Multiplication, Addition, Subtraction

The magician will tell how many pennies have been left on the table.

Trick 21. Square Coins: Multiplication (Squaring), Subtraction, Addition, Division

The magician will be able to tell how much money is picked up from a pile of mixed coins.

✳ ✳ ✳ ✳ ✳ ✳ ✳ ✳ ✳ ✳

Teacher Script

You're going to learn some tricks using money. In some of the tricks, we may be using an overhead projector so that everyone can see what is happening with the coins. These tricks involve laying coins out on a table and it will be easier for the audience to know what is happening if they see what you're doing projected on a wall.

Pocket Change to Spare: Multiplication, Addition, Subtraction

Explanation to the audience: **I will be able to tell you how much spare change you have.**

THE PROPS

a dark-colored marker

a large piece of paper

THE TRICK

1. Ask for a volunteer who has spare change with a value that is under one dollar.
2. Give the volunteer the marker and put on your blindfold.
3. Instruction to the volunteer: **Write down the amount of spare change you have.**
4. Instruction to the volunteer: **Multiply that number by 2. Then add 6.**
5. Instruction to the volunteer: **Multiply the answer by 5 and tell me the answer.**
6. In your mind, cross out the number in the ones place, subtract 3, and you are left with the amount of money the volunteer started with.

THE MAGIC

Why does this work?

Multiplying a number by 2 and then multiplying it by 5 is just like multiplying it by 10. You end up with the number followed by a zero. In this trick 6 is added and then multiplied by 5. Five times 6 is 30. Since the number in the ones place doesn't affect our answer, you cross out the ones place number in the answer the volunteer gives you and in the 30. Subtract 3 from the remaining number and you know how much money the volunteer has.

Example:

The volunteer has 37 cents and doubles that amount:	37 x 2 = 74
He or she adds 6 and multiplies the answer by 5:	74 + 6 = 80 and 80 x 5 = 400
Cross out the last number and subtract 3:	40 – 3 = 37 cents

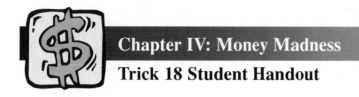
Pocket Change to Spare:
Multiplication, Addition, Subtraction

Name _____ Date _____

Now you try it:

1. Lay out some spare change as long as its value is less than one dollar.

2. Multiply the amount by 2.

3. Add 6.

4. Multiply the answer by 5.

5. Cross out the number in the ones place and subtract 3.

6. You are right back at the amount of money you had in the beginning.

How did you do?

Materials (What props did you use?)

Procedure (How did you do the trick?)

Conclusion (What makes the magic work?)

Equations (What equations did you use to make the magic work?)

Variation

Try this trick with change over one dollar. Start with 137 cents and follow the pattern of the trick. Does the math magic work in the same way? Do the work on the back of this paper.

Money Piles:
Multiplication, Addition, Subtraction

Explanation to the audience: **Without looking, I will tell you how many pennies are in two piles you make.**

THE PROPS

20 pennies

an overhead projector

a dark-colored marker

a large piece of paper

THE TRICK

1. Give a volunteer the marker and put on your blindfold.
2. Instruction to the volunteer: **Make two piles of pennies with the same or different number of pennies in each pile.**
3. Instruction to the volunteer: **Now multiply the number of pennies in the first pile by 5 and add 3.**
4. Instruction to the volunteer: **Multiply your answer by 4 and add 11.**
5. Instruction to the volunteer: **Multiply the answer by 5 and add the number of pennies from the second pile.**
6. Instruction to the volunteer: **Tell me your answer and I will tell you how many pennies you have in each pile.**
7. You subtract 115 from the number given to you. The number in the hundreds column and above will give you the number of pennies in the first pile; the numbers in the tens and ones places will give you then number of pennies in the second pile.
8. Say some magic words and reveal how many pennies are in each pile.

THE MAGIC

Why does this work?

Multiplying the number of coins in the first pile by 5 and then 4 and then 5 again is just like multiplying it by 10 twice. You end up with the number of coins followed by two zeroes.

Example:

12 x 5 = 60; 60 x 4 = 240; 240 x 5 = 1,200

The volunteer adds the number of coins in the second pile to 1,200 right where the zeroes are. You add the other numbers to trick the volunteer.

The numbers you add total 115 after they are multiplied along with the number of coins.

Example:

3 x 4 = 12; 12 + 11 = 23; 23 x 5 = 115

So all you have to do is subtract 115 and you have the number of coins in each pile.

Example:

12 pennies in pile one and 8 pennies in pile two.

Multiply the coins in the first pile by 5 and add 3:   12 x 5 = 60; 60 + 3 = 63

Multiply the answer by 4 and add 11:   63 x 4 = 252; 252 + 11 = 263

Multiply that answer by 5 and add the
  number of coins in the other pile: 263 x 5 = 1,315; 1,315 + 8 = 1,323

Subtract 115:   1,323 – 115 = 1,208

12 pennies in the first pile; 8 pennies in the second pile!

Money Piles:
Multiplication, Addition, Subtraction

Name _____ Date _____

Now you try it:

1. Make two piles of pennies with the same or different number of pennies in each pile.
2. Now multiply the number of pennies in the first pile by 5 and add 3.
3. Multiply your answer by 4 and add 11.
4. Multiply the answer by 5 and add the number of pennies from the second pile.
5. Subtract 115 from the final answer. The number in the hundreds column and above will be the number of pennies in the first pile and the numbers in the tens and one places will be the number of coins in the second pile.

How did you do?

Materials (What props did you use?)

Procedure (How did you do the trick?)

Conclusion (What makes the magic work?)

Equations (What equations did you use to do make the magic work?)

Variation

Try adding different numbers. Add 5 and 13 instead of 3 and 11. What will you subtract to make the magic work? Do the work on the back of this paper.

Hide and Seek:
Multiplication, Addition, Subtraction

Explanation to the audience: **After someone takes some coins away from the pile of money here, I will correctly guess how much money is left.**

THE PROPS
20 pennies
an overhead projector
a dark-colored marker
a large piece of paper

THE TRICK

1. Put the 20 pennies on the overhead projector.
2. Turn your back and ask a volunteer to take any number of coins from the pile of coins.
3. Instruction to the volunteer: **Double the number of pennies that are left, add 4, and multiply the answer by 5.**
4. Instruction to the volunteer: **Now add 12 to the answer and multiply the number by 10.**
5. Instruction to the volunteer: **Tell me your final answer.**
6. In your mind, or using a pad and pencil, subtract 320 and cross off the last two digits. You will have the number of coins left on the projector.

THE MAGIC

Why does this work?

The volunteer doubles the number of pennies, then multiplies the answer by 5 and later by 10. That gives him or her the number of pennies followed by two zeroes.

Example:

4 pennies doubled to 8; 8 x 5 = 40; 40 x 10 = 400

The numbers added total 320 when multiplied along with the number of pennies.

Example:

Add 4 and multiply by 5:   4 x 5 = 20

Add 12 and multiply by 10:   20 + 12 = 32; 32 x 10 = 320

So all you have to do is subtract 320 and cross off the last two zeroes to get the number of pennies on the projector.

Example:

18 pennies are left on the projector.

18 doubled is 36.

Add 4 and multiply by 5:   36 + 4 = 40; 40 x 5 = 200

Add 12 and multiply by 10:   200 + 12 = 212; 212 x 10 = 2,120

Subtract 320:   2,120 – 320 = 1,800

Cross out the zeroes and you end up with the original 18 pennies that were left on the projector.

Hide and Seek:
Multiplication, Addition, Subtraction

Name _____ Date _____

Now you try it:

1. Lay out 20 pennies on a table.
2. Take any number of pennies from the pile.
3. Double the number of pennies that are left on the table, add 4, and multiply by 5.
4. Now add 12 to the answer and multiply the number by 10.
5. Subtract 320 from the final answer and cross off the last two digits. You will have the number of pennies left on the table.

How did you do?

Materials (What props did you use?)

Procedure (How did you do the trick?)

Conclusion (What makes the magic work?)

Equations (What equations did you use to make the magic work?)

Variation

Change this trick to say that you will tell how many pennies the person took from the pile. Have him or her use that number throughout the trick, follow the pattern, and you have another trick. Do the work on the back of this paper.

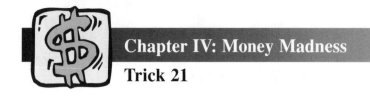

Square Coins: Multiplication (Squaring), Subtraction, Addition, Division

Explanation to the audience: **I will be able to tell you how much money you pick up from the pile of coins I have here.**

PROPS

a pile of mixed coins under one dollar

a dark-colored marker

a large piece of paper

THE TRICK

1. Give the volunteer the marker and put on your blindfold.
2. Tell him or her to pick up as many coins as he or she wants and to write the amount of money he or she has on the paper.
3. Ask him to square that number. (To square a number you multiply it by itself.)
4. Instruction to the volunteer: **Subtract one cent from your original amount and square that number too.**
5. Instruction to the volunteer: **Subtract the smaller one from the larger one and tell me the difference.**
6. In your mind, add 1 to the number the volunteer gives you and divide the answer by 2 to get the amount of money he or she chose from the pile of coins.

THE MAGIC

Why does this work?

You tell the volunteer to subtract one cent so he or she will get an amount of money consecutive to the amount of money he or she picked. Consecutive numbers are one number apart. When you square any two consecutive numbers and subtract the smaller answer from the larger, the result is the larger number doubled less one.

Example:

6 squared is 36 and 5 squared is 25: $36 - 25 = 11$

11 is one less than 6 doubled. You add one to get the original number doubled and then divide by 2 to undo the doubling.

Example:

Volunteer picks 32 cents: 32 squared is 1,024

Subtract one cent from his or her amount leaving 31 cents.

31 squared is 961: $1,024 - 961 = 63$

$63 + 1 = 64$: $64 \div 2 = 32$

You are back at the original amount of money.

Square Coins: Multiplication (Squaring), Subtraction, Addition, Division

Name _____ Date _____

Now you try it:

1. Choose an amount of money. Square the number.
2. Subtract 1 from the original amount and square that number too.
3. Subtract the smaller amount from the larger amount. Add 1 to the result and divide the answer by 2. Are you back to your original amount of money? You should be.

How did you do?

Materials (What props did you use?)

Procedure (How did you do the trick?)

Conclusion (What makes the magic work?)

Equations (What equations did you use to make the magic work?)

Variation

Try this trick with 14 and 15; 29 and 30; and 225 and 226. Follow the formula:

Square two consecutive numbers, subtract the smaller answer from the larger, add one to the result, and divide that number in half. Does this always work? Do your work on the other side of this paper.

Chapter V
X+Y=MAGIC

* * * * * * * * * * *

Teacher Notes

The tricks in this chapter are built on algebraic equations and serve as an introduction to the study of algebra. The actual tricks use formulas that have been used throughout the previous chapters and should be familiar to the students.

Trick 22. Knowing the Unknown: Multiplication, Addition, Subtraction

The magician will tell the value of all the numbers in an equation. This is the most difficult of the tricks in this chapter as it entails finding all three numbers in an equation made up by a volunteer.

Trick 23. A Double Dose: Multiplication, Addition, Subtraction, Division

The magician will be able to tell the value of both x and y in this equation involving addition.

Trick 24. X Marks the Spot: Multiplication, Addition, Division, Subtraction

In this algebraic equation involving multiplication, the magician will discover the value of x and the answer to the equation.

Trick 25. Minus the Magic: Addition, Multiplication, Division, Subtraction,

The magician will be able to tell the value of both x and y in this equation involving subtraction.

Teacher Script

We are going to be learning some tricks that involve using algebraic equations. We will be using some of the same magic techniques we've already learned to find secret numbers and, once we've "magically" learned those numbers, we will go on to solve the algebraic equation using plain old number knowledge.

Knowing the Unknown: Multiplication, Addition, Subtraction

Explanation to the audience: **I will be able to tell the value of all three numbers in an equation even though I won't know what values you have assigned to them.**

THE PROPS
a dark-colored marker, a large piece of paper

THE TRICK
1. Write this algebraic equation on the paper: x + y = ?
2. Give the volunteer the marker and turn your back. You may want to read the directions for this trick and use a pad and pencil to get the answers.
3. Instruction to the volunteer: **Decide on the value of the variables. Example: x = 14 and y = 14.**
4. Instruction to the volunteer: **Write the first variable down. Multiply it by 5.**
5. Instruction to the volunteer: **Add 8. Then double the number. Tell me the answer.**
6. In your mind, cross off the number in the ones place, subtract 1 from the answer and you will have the first variable. Write it down.
7. Instruction to the volunteer: **Write the second variable. Double it and add 4.**
8. Instruction to the volunteer: **Multiply the answer by 5 and add 4 again.**
9. In your mind, cross out the number in the ones place, subtract 2 from the answer to get the second variable. Once you have the two variables, add them, and you have the entire equation.

THE MAGIC
Why does this work?
To find the value of the variables, you have the volunteer double and multiply them by 5. This leaves each variable with a zero after it. So you do not have to be concerned with the number in the ones place for either number.

Variable One: You doubled 8 giving you 16. Since you don't have to worry about the number in the ones place, cross out the 6 in the number 16, and cross out the number in the ones place in the answer. Subtract the 1 that is left from the 16.

Variable Two: This number was doubled and multiplied by 5 and 24 was added in all (4 times 5 plus 4). You cross out the number in the ones place and subtract 2 (the number in the tens place of 24) to get the second variable. Add the two variables and you have the entire equation.

Example: x + y = 14; 8 + 6 = 14

First Variable:	8	Second Variable:	6
Multiply by 5:	5 x 8 = 40	Double:	6 x 2 = 12
Add 5:	40 + 5 = 45	Add 4:	12 + 4 = 16
Double:	45 x 2 = 90	Multiply by 5:	16 x 5 = 80
Cross out the zero and subtract 1		Add 4:	80 + 4 = 84
9 − 1 = 8, the first variable		Cross out the 4 and subtract 2: 8 − 2 = 6, the second variable	

Add the two variables to get the entire equation. The entire equation is 8 + 6 = 14.

Knowing the Unknown: Multiplication, Addition, Subtraction

Name _____ Date _____

Now you try it:

1. Write any algebraic equation you wish adding two variables.

   Example: 11 + 7 = 18

2. Write the first variable down. Multiply it by 5.

3. Add 8. Then double the number.

4. Cross off the number in the ones place, subtract 1 from the answer and you will have the first variable. Write it down.

5. Write the second variable. Double it and add 4.

6. Multiply the answer by 5 and add 4 again.

7. Cross out the number in the ones place, subtract 2 from the answer to get the second variable. Once you have the two variables, add them and you have the entire equation.

How did you do?

Materials (What props did you use?)

Procedure (How did you do the trick?)

Conclusion (What makes the magic work?)

Equations (What equations did you use to make the magic work?)

A Double Dose: Multiplication, Addition, Subtraction, Division

Explanation to the audience: I will be able to tell the value of both x and y in this equation involving addition.

THE PROPS
a dark-colored marker, a large piece of paper

THE TRICK
1. Write the equation x + y = 28 on the paper.
2. Give the volunteer the marker and put on your blindfold.
3. Ask the volunteer to assign values to both x and y. When added, they must equal 28.
4. Instruction to the volunteer: **Choose one of the numbers and double it.**
5. Instruction to the volunteer: **Now add 20 to your answer and double it again.**
6. Instruction to the volunteer: **The last thing for you to do is to divide your answer by 4 and tell me your final answer.**
7. In your mind, subtract 10 from the number given to you and you will have the value of one of the numbers in the equation.
8. Since you know the answer in this equation, you subtract the value you have just discovered from 28 and you will have both variables and the complete equation.

THE MAGIC
You know the answer in this equation, so once you know one of the variables, you subtract it from the answer to discover the second variable.

Why does this work?
The volunteer doubles the first variable, doubles it again and divides it by 4, bringing him or her back to the number he or she started with.

Example: 5 doubled is 10, doubled again is 20, divided by 4 is 5.
The 20 you told him or her to add is doubled making 40, then divided by 4, leaving 10.
You subtract 10 to give you the amount of the first variable.

Example: 12 + 16 = 28 is the starting equation.

Double one of the variables:	12 x 2 = 24
Add 20 to the answer:	24 + 20 = 44
Double the answer:	44 + 44 = 88
Divide the answer by 4:	88 ÷ 4 = 22

You subtract 10 to give you 12, the first variable.
28 – 12 = 16
The original equation was 12 + 16 = 28.

A Double Dose: Multiplication, Addition, Subtraction, Division

Name _____ Date _____

Now you try it:

1. Write an equation where the two variables equal 28.
2. Choose one of the numbers and double it.
3. Add 20 to your answer and double it again.
4. Divide the answer by 4 and subtract 10 to get the value of one of the numbers in the equation. Subtract that value from 28 and you will have both variables and the complete equation.

How did you do?

Materials (What props did you use?)

Procedure (How did you do the trick?)

Conclusion (What makes the magic work?)

Equations (What equations did you use to make the magic work?)

Variation

Try this trick again with this equation: x + y = 47

Do the work on the back of this paper.

X Marks the Spot: Multiplication, Addition, Division, Subtraction

Explanation to the audience: **In this algebraic equation involving multiplication, I will know the value of x and the answer to the equation.**

THE PROPS

a dark-colored marker

a large piece of paper

THE TRICK

1. Write this equation on the paper: $5x + 4x = ?$
2. Give a volunteer the marker and put on your blindfold.
3. Instruction to the volunteer: **Assign a value for x and solve the equation. Write it down.**

   For instance, if x is to equal 4, then the volunteer will write $20 + 16 = 36$.

   ($5 \times 4 = 20$ and $4 \times 4 = 16$)
4. Instruction to the volunteer: **Double all numbers in the equation.**
5. Instruction to the volunteer: **Add 30 to each number.**
6. Instruction to the volunteer: **Divide all numbers by 2 and tell me the three numbers.**
7. In your mind, subtract 15 from each number. Say some magic words and reveal the volunteer's original equation.

THE MAGIC

Why does this work?

After adding 30 to the numbers, they are divided by 2. Thirty divided by 2 equals 15. The volunteer is left with his or her original numbers because the numbers were doubled and then were divided in half and half of 30 is 15. When you subtract 15 you have his or her original equation.

> **Example:**
>
> x = 4
>
> $5 \times 4 = 20$ and $4 \times 4 = 16$
>
> $20 + 16 = 36$
>
> | Double all numbers: | 40, 32, 72 |
> | Add 30 to each number: | 70, 62, 102 |
> | Divide each number by 2: | 35, 31, 51 |
> | Subtract 15 from each: | $20 + 16 = 36$ |
>
> You are back at the original equation.

X Marks the Spot: Multiplication, Addition, Division, Subtraction

Name _____ Date _____

Now you try it:

1. Choose a value for x in the equation $5x + 4x = ?$
2. Double each number.
3. Add 30 to each number.
4. Divide the numbers by 2.
5. Now you subtract 15 from each answer. You now know the original equation.

How did you do?

Materials (What props did you use?)

Procedure (How did you do the trick?)

Conclusion (What makes the magic work?)

Equations (What equations did you use to make the magic work?)

Variation

How do you find the original value of x? Since 5x equals 20, you divide 5 into 20 to find the value of x. Determine the value of x in these equations: $4x = 16$; $3x = 72$; $6x = 36$; $9x = 81$; and $12x = 84$. Do the work on the back of this paper.

Minus the Magic: Addition, Multiplication, Division, Subtraction

Explanation to the audience: **I will be able to tell the value of both x and y in this equation involving subtraction.**

THE PROPS

a large piece of paper

a dark-colored marker

THE TRICK

1. Write this equation on the paper: $x - y = 25$
2. Give the volunteer the marker and put on your blindfold.
3. Instruction to the volunteer: **Make up any values for x and y that make sense. Both numbers must equal 25.**
4. Instruction to the volunteer: **Add 10 to the first number in the equation, the value of x.**
5. Instruction to the volunteer: **Multiply the answer by 4.**
6. Instruction to the volunteer: **Divide that answer by 2 and tell me the final number you reach.**
7. In your mind, divide the number given to you by 2 and subtract 10 to give you the value of x. Subtract the answer of the equation from the value of x to get the value of y.
8. Say some magic words and reveal to the audience the entire equation.

THE MAGIC

Why does this work?

Ten is added to the first variable before it is multiplied by 4 and then divided by 2 ($4 \times 10 = 40$; $40 \div 2 = 20$).

When you divide the answer by 2, you are dividing the 20 also ($20 \div 2 = 10$).

Now you are left with 10, which you subtract to get the original number, the value of x.

Once you know the value of x, you subtract it from the answer in the equation to get the value of y.

Example:

$45 - 20 = 25$ is the original equation.

Add 10 to the value of x:	$45 + 10 = 55$
Multiply that number by 4:	$4 \times 55 = 220$
Divide the answer by 2:	$220 \div 2 = 110$

Divide that answer by 2 and subtract 10 to find the value of x.

You know that $45 - y = 25$, so the value of y is easy to find.

$45 - 25 = 20$. The value of y is 20.

The original equation reads:	$45 - 20 = 25$

Minus the Magic: Addition, Multiplication, Division, Subtraction

Name _____ Date _____

Now you try it:

1. Choose values for x and y in this equation: $x - y = 17$.
2. Add 10 to the value of x.
3. Multiply that number by 4.
4. Divide the answer by 2.
5. Divide the answer by 2 again and subtract 10.
6. You now will have the value of x. Subtract that number from 17 to get the value of y.
7. Write your equation. Is it the same as the one you started with?

How did you do?

Materials (What props did you use?)

Procedure (How did you do the trick?)

Conclusion (What makes the magic work?)

Equations (What equations did you use to make the magic work?)

Chapter VI
MIXED UP MAGIC

✷ ✷ ✷ ✷ ✷ ✷ ✷ ✷ ✷ ✷
Teacher Notes

Here are several tricks that don't fit into any of the categories of the first chapters.

Trick 26. I Know Where You Live! Addition, Multiplication, Division
The magician will be able to tell someone his or her address.

Trick 27. Magic Multiples: Multiplication, Division
A volunteer will choose a secret number and multiply it by another secret number, but the magician will be able to tell him or her the original number.

Trick 28. What Time Did You Say? Multiplication, Addition, Division, Subtraction
The magician will tell someone what his or her favorite time of the afternoon is.

Trick 29. Fractured Fractions: Multiplication, Addition, Subtraction
The magician will be able to tell what fraction was written.

Trick 30. Act Your Age: Addition, Subtraction
The magician will tell a volunteer his or her age.

Trick 31. Age Old Magic: Multiplication, Addition, Subtraction
The magician will be able to tell someone his or her age and the number he or she secretly chose.

Trick 32. Cross Out: Multiplication, Addition, Subtraction
The magician will know what number was crossed out from a secret number.

✷ ✷ ✷ ✷ ✷ ✷ ✷ ✷ ✷ ✷
Teacher Script

Here are more tricky tricks that use a lot of the magic ways to do math that we have already learned. We'll just use paper and marker to perform our magic in these tricks.

I Know Where You Live!
Addition, Multiplication, Division

Explanation to the audience: You are going to start with the numbers in your address and the addresses of your neighbors and change them by doing some math work. No matter what you do, I will be able to tell what your address is.

THE PROPS
a dark-colored marker

a large piece of paper

THE TRICK

1. Put the paper where the audience can see what is being written on it. Turn your back and ask a volunteer to write the numbers from his or her street address on the paper.

2. Instruction to the volunteer: **Now add 4 to your address to get the number of your neighbor's street address and subtract 4 from your address to get the address of the neighbor who lives on the other side of you. Add the three street addresses together.**

3. Instruction to the volunteer: **Multiply the answer by 2.**

4. Instruction to the volunteer: **Now divide your answer by 3.**

5. Instruction to the volunteer: **Tell me your final answer and I will tell you what your address is.**

6. After you say your magic words, reveal the final answer. It will be the number you get when you divide the number the volunteer gives you in half.

THE MAGIC
This trick relies on averaging to get the right answer.

Why does this work?

The volunteer adds three evenly spaced numbers. You know that when you divide that number by 3, you will get the middle number, which is his or her address. He or she has doubled the number so, when you divide it in half, which is the opposite of doubling, you get his or her address.

Example:

The volunteer's address is 749.

The addresses before and after are 745 and 753.

$749 + 745 + 753 = 2,247$

2247 doubled is 4,494; 4,494 divided by 3 is 1,498.

Half of 1,498 is 749, the address of the volunteer.

I Know Where You Live!
Addition, Multiplication, Division

Name _____ Date _____

Now you try it:

1. Write down your street number.
2. Find the addresses before and after your address by adding and subtracting 4 from your street number and add the three numbers.
3. Multiply your answer by 2.
4. Divide the answer by 3.
5. Split that answer in half and you will have your address back again!

How did you do?

Materials (What props did you use?)

Procedure (How did you do the trick?)

Conclusion (What makes the trick work?)

Equations (What equations did you use to make the magic work?)

Variation

Try this trick with several addresses, both long and short. Does it work the same no matter how long or short the address is? Can you explain why? Do the work on the back of this paper.

Magic Multiples: Multiplication, Division

Explanation to the audience: **You're going to pick a secret number and multiply it by any number you want and I will tell you what your original number was.**

THE PROPS

a dark-colored marker

a large piece of paper

THE TRICK

1. Put on your blindfold and ask a volunteer to write a number on the paper.
2. Tell the volunteer to multiply that number by any number he or she chooses.
3. Then tell him or her to multiply the answer by 2.
4. Instruction to the volunteer: **Divide your answer by the first multiplier.**
5. Ask him or her to tell you his or her answer. Divide it by 2 and you will have his or her original number.

THE MAGIC

Why does this work?

Multiplication and division are opposites. The volunteer multiplies the original number he or she chose by another number and divides it by the same number. This brings him or her back to his or her original number. Then he or she doubles that number. All you have to do is divide the number by 2 to get the number he or she chose.

Example:

Choose 6.

Multiply it by any number you wish.

Say we choose 8: $8 \times 6 = 48$

Multiply it by 2: $48 \times 2 = 96$

Divide it by the first multiplier, which was 8: $96 \div 8 = 12$

You divide the answer by 2 and get 6, the number chosen in Step 1.

Magic Multiples: Multiplication, Division

Name _____ Date _____

Now you try it:
1. Choose a number.
2. Multiply it by any number you choose and then multiply the answer by 2.
3. Divide the answer by the first multiplier.
4. Divide that answer by 2 and you will end up with the original number you chose.

How did you do?
Materials (What props did you use?)

Procedure (How did you do the trick?)

Conclusion (What makes the magic work?)

Equations (What equations did you use to make the trick work?)

Variation
Here's another similar trick. Pick an even number. Divide it by any number that will go into it evenly. Multiply the answer by 5. Then multiply the result by the first divisor. To get back to the original number, you need to divide the answer by 5. Try this new trick on the back of this paper.

What Time Did You Say? Multiplication, Addition, Division, Subtraction

Explanation to the audience: **In this trick, I will be able to tell you what your favorite hour is.**

THE PROPS

a clock

a large piece of paper

a dark-colored marker

THE TRICK

1. Give a volunteer the marker and put on your blindfold.

2. Instruction to the volunteer: **Look at the clock and pick your favorite hour between 1 and 8 o'clock. Write that number and double it.**

3. Instruction to the volunteer: **There are 60 seconds in a minute. Add 60 to your number.**

4. Instruction to the volunteer: **There are 60 minutes in an hour. Add 60 again.**

5. Instruction to the volunteer: **There are 24 hours in a day. Add 24 to your last answer.**

6. Instruction to the volunteer: **Split your final answer in half.**

7. Instruction to the volunteer: **Tell me the answer and I will tell you your favorite time of day.**

8. Subtract 2 from the final answer, and the hour the volunteer chose as his or her favorite time of day will be the number in the ones place.

THE MAGIC

Why does this work?

You only need to think about the ones column to make this trick work because you know a single digit number was chosen. The volunteer adds 4 to the ones column during the entire trick. Then he or she splits the number in half. Half of 4 is 2. So when you subtract 2 from the final answer, the time he or she chose will be the number in the ones place.

Example:

The person's favorite hour is 8, and 8 doubled is 16.

60 seconds is added.	$60 + 16 = 76$
60 minutes is added.	$76 + 60 = 136$
24 hours is added.	$136 + 24 = 160$
160 is split in half to 80.	$80 - 2 = 78$

Cross out the number in the tens place and you have the volunteer's favorite hour.

What Time Did You Say? Multiplication, Addition, Division, Subtraction

Name _____ Date _____

Now you try it:

1. Pick your favorite hour between 1 and 8 o'clock and write that number down. Double it.

2. There are 60 seconds in a minute, so add 60 to your answer.

3. There are 60 minutes in an hour, so add 60 again.

4. There are 24 hours in a day, so add 24. Split the answer in half.

5. Now subtract 2 from the answer, cross out the digit in the tens place, and you will have the time you picked in the first place.

How did you do?

Materials (What props did you use?)

Procedure (How did you do the trick?)

Conclusion (What makes the magic work?)

Equations (What equations did you use to make the trick work?)

Variation

Here's a similar trick: Pick an hour between 1 and 8 o'clock and add 60 twice. Then add 24, and 7 (for 7 days in the week), and 52 (for 52 weeks in the year). To get back to the original time, subtract 3 and cross out the number in the hundreds place. To understand how this works, determine what was added to the original number in the ones place. Do the work on the back of this paper.

Fractured Fractions:
Multiplication, Addition, Subtraction

Explanation to the audience: **You will write a fraction and I will be able to tell you what fraction you wrote.**

THE PROPS
a dark-colored marker, a large piece of paper

THE TRICK
1. Give a volunteer the marker and put on your blindfold.
2. Instruction to the volunteer: **Write a simple fraction on the paper with none of the digits over 9.**
3. Instruction to the volunteer: **Multiply the numerator by 5 and add 6.**
4. Instruction to the volunteer: **Double that number.**
5. Introduction to the volunteer: **Now add the denominator and tell me the answer. I will tell you what fraction you wrote.**
6. In your mind, subtract 12 from the number the volunteer gives you and use the first number in your answer for the numerator and the second number for the denominator. That will be the fraction that was written in the first place.

THE MAGIC
You will always get the numbers of the original fraction when you subtract 12 from the volunteer's final answer. The first number will be the numerator and the second will be the denominator.

Why does this work?
The numerator was multiplied by 5 and was then doubled. That is just like multiplying it by 10. When a number is multiplied by 10, you will always have the original number with a zero after it.

   Example:
   6 x 5 = 30, and 30 doubled is 60.
   When the denominator is added, you have the number of the numerator and the number of the denominator.
   The trick is in adding a 6. Six doubled is 12 so when you subtract 12 the two digits left are the numerator and denominator of the original fraction.

   Example:

Original fraction:	6/7
Multiply the numerator by 5:	5 x 6 = 30
Add 6:	30 + 6 = 36
Double the answer:	36 doubled is 72
Add the denominator:	72 + 7 = 79
Subtract 12:	79 – 12 = 67

   6 is the numerator and 7 is the denominator: 6/7
   You're back to the original fraction!

Fractured Fractions: Multiplication, Addition, Subtraction

Name _____ Date _____

Now you try it:

1. Write a fraction on the paper.
2. Multiply the numerator by 5 and add 6.
3. Double that number and add the denominator.
4. Subtract 12 from the answer.
5. The first number in your answer is the numerator and the second is the denominator.

How did you do?

Materials (What props did you use?)

Procedure (How did you do the trick?)

Conclusion (What makes the magic work?)

Equations (What equations did you use to make the trick work?)

Variation

Try the trick this way. Write a fraction with a double digit numerator and denominator. Example: 25/30. Multiply the numerator by 50, add 60, and double the answer. Then add the denominator. Subtract 120 from the answer to get the original fraction. Do the work on the back of this paper.

Act Your Age: Addition, Subtraction

Explanation to the audience: **I will be able to tell you how old you are after you do a little math work.**

THE PROPS

a dark-colored marker

a large piece of paper

THE TRICK

1. Give a volunteer the marker and put on your blindfold.
2. Instruction to the volunteer: **Write your age on the paper.**
3. Instruction to the volunteer: **There are 31 days in seven months, so add the number 31.**
4. Instruction to the volunteer: **There are 30 days in four months, so add 30.**
5. Instruction to the volunteer: **There are 28 days in February, so add 28.**
6. Instruction to the volunteer: **There are 12 months in a year, so add the number 12 to your answer.**
7. Instruction to the volunteer: **There are 10 years in a decade, so add 10.**
8. Instruction to the volunteer: **There are 100 years in a century, so add 100. Tell me your answer and I will tell you how old you are.**
9. In your mind subtract 11 from the remaining number and cross out the number in the hundreds place. The answer will be the volunteer's age.

THE MAGIC

We do not use the number in the hundreds place to get the volunteer's age because the ages you are working with will have either one or two digits. Just make sure you don't do this trick with anyone who is 100 years old or older!

How does this work?

The volunteer adds 31, 30, 28, 12, 10, and 100 to his or her age. Those numbers add up to 211. After you subtract 11 from the number the volunteer tells you and cross out the number in the hundreds place, you will have his or her age.

Example:

The volunteer is 16.

16 + 31 = 47

47 + 30 = 77

77 + 28 = 105

105 + 12 = 117

117 + 10 = 127

127 + 100 = 227

227 – 11 = 216

Cross out the number in the hundreds place and you have the volunteer's age.

Act Your Age: Addition, Subtraction

Name _____ Date _____

Now you try it:

1. Write your age on the paper.
2. There are 31 days in seven months, so add the number 31.
3. There are 30 days in four months, so add 30.
4. There are 28 days in February, so add 28.
5. There are 12 months in a year, so add the number 12 to your answer.
6. There are 10 years in a decade, so add 10. There are 100 years in a century, so add 100.
7. Subtract 11 and cross out the number in the hundreds place. You are back at the age written in Step 1.

How did you do?

Materials (What props did you use?)

Procedure (How did you do the trick?)

Conclusion (What makes the magic work?)

Equations (What equations did you use to make the magic work?)

Variation

What parts of this trick could you leave out and still make it work? Try it leaving out various parts to make new tricks. Do the work on the back of this paper.

Age Old Magic:
Multiplication, Addition, Subtraction

Explanation to the audience: **Here's another way for me to tell your age and a secret number you chose.**

THE PROPS

a large piece of paper, a dark-colored marker, a small pad and pencil

THE TRICK

1. Give the volunteer the marker and turn your back.
2. Instruction to the volunteer: **Pick any number from 1 to 9 and write it.**
3. Instruction to the volunteer: **Double the number and add 5.**
4. Instruction to the volunteer: **Now multiply the answer by 50 and add the number of this year.**
5. Instruction to the volunteer: **Now subtract the year of your birth.**
6. Instruction to the volunteer: **Tell me the answer to all your work and I will tell you your age at the end of this year and the number you chose.**
7. In your mind or using a pad and paper, subtract 250. The first number in your answer will be the number he or she chose and the other number or numbers will be his or her age.

THE MAGIC

Why does this work?

The current year minus the year of someone's birth, gives us his or her age by the end of the year.

Example:

$2003 - 1991 = 12$

The secret number is doubled and then multiplied by 50, which is just like multiplying it by 100 ($2 \times 50 = 100$), giving the volunteer's number with two zeros after it. When she or he adds her or his age, it goes in the space where the two zeros are. The number 5 was added and multiplied by 50 ($5 \times 50 = 250$). So when you subtract 250 you have the correct numbers to tell him or her.

Example:

A 65-year-old volunteer picks the number 5.

Doubles the number:	$5 \times 2 = 10$
Adds 5:	$10 + 5 = 15$
Multiplies by 50:	$15 \times 50 = 750$
Adds the current year:	$750 + 2003 = 2753$
Subtracts the year of his or her birth:	$2753 - 1938 = 815$
You subtract 250:	$815 - 250 = 565$

5 is the number chosen and 65 is the age of the volunteer.

Age Old Magic:
Multiplication, Addition, Subtraction

Name _____ Date _____

Now you try it:

1. Pick a number from 1 to 9.
2. Double the number and add 5.
3. Multiply by 50 and add the current year.
4. Subtract the year of your birth.
5. Subtract 250.
6. The first number is the number you picked and the rest is your age at the end of this year. Right?

How did you do?

Materials (What props did you use?)

Procedure (How did you do the trick?)

Conclusion (What makes the magic work?)

Equations (What equations did you use to make the magic work?)

Variation

Try this trick with a double-digit secret number and a triple-digit secret number. Does it work the same way? Do the work on the back of this paper.

Cross Out:
Multiplication, Addition, Subtraction

Explanation to the audience: **I am going to tell you what digit you cross out from a secret number.**

THE PROPS

a dark-colored marker

a large piece of paper

THE TRICK

1. Tell a volunteer to pick a number and multiply it by 100.
2. Instruction to the volunteer: **Add 36 and then subtract the original number.**
3. Instruction to the volunteer: **Cross out 1 digit from your answer. Tell me all the digits left in your answer.**
4. You add all the digits the volunteer gives you and subtract the total from the next highest multiple of 9. Your answer will be the digit that was crossed out.

THE MAGIC

Why does this work?

First, the original number is multiplied by 100. That gives you the number plus 2 zeroes.

Example:

$12 \times 100 = 1,200$

Then you add a multiple of 9 (36) and it takes the place of the two zeroes after the original number.

Example:

$1,200 + 36 = 1,236$

When you subtract the original number, the digits in the answer will total 9. (This only happens when you add any multiple of nine.) One digit is crossed out and the remaining digits are added. You know all the digits must add up to a multiple of 9. You add the remaining digits and subtract the sum from the next highest multiple of 9 and you will have the digit that was crossed out.

Example:

Pick 75

$75 \times 100 = 7,500$

Add 36: $7,500 + 36 = 7,536$

Subtract the original number: $7,536 - 75 = 7,461$

$7 + 4 + 6 + 1 = 18$

Cross out the 6 and you are left with $7 + 4 + 1 = 12$.

You subtract 12 from the next highest multiple of 9, which is 18.

$18 - 12 = 6$, the crossed out number.

If the answer given to you is a multiple of 9, then the number crossed out was a zero!

Cross Out:
Multiplication, Addition, Subtraction

Name _____ Date _____

Now you try it:

1. Pick a number and multiply it by 100.

2. Add 36 and then subtract the original number.

3. Cross out 1 digit from your answer.

4. Add all the digits that are left and subtract the total from the next highest multiple of 9. Your answer will be the digit that was crossed out.

How did you do?

Materials (What props did you use?)

Procedure (How did you do the trick?)

Conclusion (What makes the magic work?)

Equations (What equations did you use to make the magic work?)

Variation

Try this trick adding other multiples of 9. Follow the pattern and try the trick adding 27, 45, and 108. Do the work on the back of this paper.

Chapter VII
THE MYSTERIOUS NUMBER NINE

* * * * * * * * * * *
Teacher Notes

In this chapter, some interesting facts about the number nine plus a few tricks that rely on the number nine to make them work are given.

Trick 33. Writing Practice: Multiplication

This trick is both amusing and instructive. The volunteer will end up writing a number over and over again.

Trick 34. Six Nines Equals What? Fractions

How to make 100 using six nines!

Trick 35. Predictably Perfect: Subtraction, Addition

Nines make the difference as the magician predicts the final answer to math work even though the problem begins with a number of the volunteer's choice.

Trick 36. Prediction Ploy: Subtraction, Addition

Using those tricky nines again, the magician will predict the final answer to math work after someone adds several numbers to the total.

Trick 37. Mysterious Facts about the Number Nine

Three mystifying facts about the number nine.

* * * * * * * * * *
Teacher Script

Here are some strange facts about the number nine and a few tricks that work because nine is so mystifying.

Why is the number nine so mysterious? It may be because it is the final number in our system of counting that can be written as a single digit. No matter how large a number is, it can only have 10 different symbols or digits: 1, 2, 3, 4, 5, 6, 7, 8, 9, 0.

After we get to the number nine, we start all over again with one and zero.

It's fun to see how numbers would work if they were in a system based on another number like 6. Then there would only be six symbols or digits that could be used to make numbers. You would count 1, 2, 3, 4, 5, 6, 11, 12, 13, 14, 15, 16, 21, and so on.

Suppose the number system were based on the number 4? How would you count?

Writing Practice: Multiplication

1. Ask a volunteer to write the numbers 1, 2, 3, 4, 5, 6, 7, 9 on a large piece of paper or on the blackboard. *Notice there is no 8.*

2. Now ask a volunteer in the audience to say what number was written the sloppiest.

3. Multiply that number by 9 and ask the volunteer to multiply the number he or she wrote by the multiple of 9 you reached. For instance if 6 is the sloppiest number, and 6 times 9 is 54, the volunteer will multiply 12,345,679 by 54.

4. Try this and see what happens. You will see why this trick is called writing practice!

Six Nines Equals What? Fractions

Here's a tricky question for you to ask your friends. Ask if they know how to put six nines together to make 100. They will probably not be able to do it, but you can.

Simply write 99 and 99/99. This equals 100 because the fraction 99/99 is the same as 1 and 99 plus 1 equals 100!

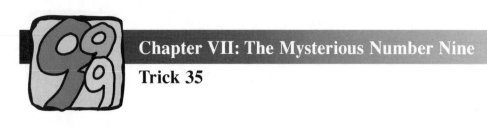

Predictably Perfect: Subtraction, Addition

Explanation to the audience: **I will predict the answer to the math work we are going to do even though you will choose the number we begin with and add other numbers you want.**

THE PROPS

a dark-colored marker, a large piece of paper, a small piece of paper

THE TRICK

1. Ask a volunteer to write any three-digit number on the paper.
2. In your mind, subtract 2 from the number he or she has written, place a 2 in front of the number and write the resulting number on a small piece of paper.

   For example, the volunteer writes: 398; subtract 2 to get 396; place a 2 in the thousandths place to get 2,396 for your prediction. Give the prediction to a member of the audience to hold.
3. Ask the volunteer to write another three-digit number below his or her first one.
4. Now you write a number under the volunteer's number. Make sure the total of his or her number and yours is 999. For example, his or her number is 461 so you add 538 to total 999.
5. Instruction to the volunteer: **Please add another three-digit number under the one I wrote.**
6. Now you write another number below his or hers to total 999 again.
7. Instruction to the volunteer: **Please add the five numbers.**
8. When the sum is reached, ask the member of the audience to read your prediction. It will be the same as the sum of the numbers.

THE MAGIC

The trick depends on your numbers added to the volunteer's numbers totaling 999.

Why does this work?

You subtract 2 from the original number and put a 2 in the thousandths place. Each time you add a number you make sure it totals 999 when added to the number the volunteer wrote. This happens twice: 999 + 999 = 1,998 1,998 is 2 less than 2,000. When you add 1,998 to the original number you get the original number plus 2,000 minus 2 which is just what you predicted.

> **Example:** Volunteer chooses a three-digit number: 742
>
> In your mind, you add a 2 in the thousandths place and subtract 2 from the new number to get 2,740. This is your prediction.
>
> | | |
> |---|---|
> | The first number: | 742 |
> | The volunteer adds a three-digit number: | 299 |
> | You add a number to his or hers to total 999: | 700 |
> | The volunteer adds a three-digit number: | 347 |
> | You add a number to his or hers to total 999: | 652 |
> | Total all the numbers: | 2,740 |
>
> You are at the number you predicted!

Predictably Perfect: Subtraction, Addition

Name _____ Date _____

Now you try it:

1. Ask someone to choose a three-digit number.

2. In your mind, you add a 2 in the thousandths place and subtract 2 from the new number. This is your prediction.

3. Ask the volunteer to add a second three-digit number.

4. You add a number to his or hers to total 999.

5. Ask the volunteer to add another three-digit number.

6. You add a number to his or hers to total 999.

7. Total the five numbers and you should be back at the number you predicted!

How did you do?

Materials (What props did you use?)

Procedure (How did you do the trick?)

Conclusion (What makes the magic work?)

Equations (What equations did you use to make the magic work?)

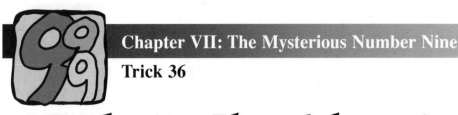

Prediction Ploy: Subtraction, Addition

Explanation to the audience: **I will predict the number we end up with even though you will add several numbers to the one we begin with.**

THE PROPS

a dark-colored marker, a large piece of paper, a small piece of paper

THE TRICK

1. Write a five-digit number that begins with a 2 on a small piece of paper and give it to a member of the audience to hold. Explanation to the audience: **This is my prediction for the answer to the math work we are going to do.**

2. In your mind, cross out the first number of your prediction, add 2 to the remaining numbers, and write that number on the large piece of paper. Choose a volunteer and give him or her the marker.

   Example: Prediction: 27,412

   Cross out the first digit: 7,412

   Add 2:   7,414

3. Instruction to the volunteer: **Write a four-digit number under my number.**

4. Then it's your turn to add a number. Make sure your number and the one the volunteer wrote add up to 9,999.

   Example: Volunteer writes 6,788 and you write 3,211 to total 9,999.

5. Repeat the last two steps. Ask the volunteer to write another four-digit number and you add one that will total 9,999 together with his or hers.

6. Instruction to the volunteer: **Now add all the numbers we have written and you will see that my prediction is correct.**

7. After the sum is reached, ask the audience member to read your prediction. It will be the same number.

THE MAGIC

This trick works because both times numbers were added, the sums totaled 9,999.

Why does this work?

To begin the trick, you remove the 2 that is in the ten thousandths place and add a 2 to your prediction number. You and the volunteer add numbers that total 9,999. This happens twice. 9,999 + 9,999 = 19,998. You added a 2 earlier. 19,998 + 2 = 20,000.

You end up replacing the 20,000 that you removed from the prediction number.

   Example: You predict the number 25,377.

   Cross out the first number and add 2 (5,377 + 2 = 5,379):   5,379

   Volunteer adds a four-digit number: 3,945

   You add a number that combined with his totals 9,999:   6,054

   Volunteer adds another four-digit number: 7,218

   You add a number that combined with his totals 9,999:   2,781

   Total the numbers: 25,377

   The sum of the numbers is the number you predicted!

Prediction Ploy: Subtraction, Addition

Name _____ Date _____

Now you try it:

1. You predict a five-digit number beginning with the number 2.
2. Cross out the first number and add 2. Write the new number down.
3. Ask someone to add a four-digit number.
4. You add a number that when combined with his or hers totals 9,999.
5. Ask someone to add another four-digit number.
6. You add a number that when combined with his or hers totals 9,999.
7. Total the numbers and you will be back at the number you predicted!

How did you do?

Materials (What props did you use?)

Procedure (How did you do the trick?)

Conclusion (What makes the magic work?)

Equations (What equations did you use to make the magic work?)

Mysterious Facts About the Number Nine

Here are some mysterious fact about the nine times table.

If you add the numbers in each product through 9 times 10 you end up with 9!

9 x 1 = 9   9 x 6 = 54 (5 + 4 = 9)

9 x 2 = 18 (1 + 8 = 9)   9 x 7 = 63 (6 + 3 = 9)

9 x 3 = 27 (2 + 7 = 9)   9 x 8 = 72 (7 + 2 = 9)

9 x 4 = 36 (3 + 6 = 9)   9 x 9 = 81 (8 + 1 = 9)

9 x 5 = 45 (4 + 5 = 9)   9 x 10 = 90 (9 + 0 = 9)

If you add some or even all of the products from the nines table together, the digits in the answer will always add up to 9!

Example:

45 + 36 = 81   and 8 + 1 = 9

81 + 90 = 171 and 1 + 7 + 1 = 9

If you reverse a number and subtract the smaller from the larger, the digits in the answer will always add up to 9.

Example: 752 – 257 = 495; 4 + 9 + 5 = 18; 1 + 8 = 9